Christian Härtel

In collaboration with the picture library of the Prussian Cultural Heritage

Berlin

A Short History

berlin edition

Bibliografische Information der Deutschen Bibliothek
Die Deutsche Bibliothek verzeichnet diese Publikation in der Deutschen Nationalbibliografie; detaillierte bibliografische Daten sind im Internet über http://dnb.ddb.de abrufbar.

2., verbesserte Auflage

Berlin-Brandenburg, 2006
KulturBrauerei Haus S
Schönhauser Allee 37, 10435 Berlin
post@bebraverlag.de
Übersetzung: Penny Croucher, London
Gesamtgestaltung: Tanja Selzer, Berlin
Schrift: Deepdene 10/13,5 pt
Druck und Bindung: Friedrich Pustet, Regensburg

ISBN 3-89809-044-2

www.bebraverlag.de

Illustrations
Archiv be.bra verlag: S. 35, 77, Back cover
Bildarchiv Preußischer Kulturbesitz, Berlin: S. 4, 7, 8 f. 11 f., 14 f., 17, 19–21, 23–29, 31 f., 36 f., 39, 41, 43, 45 f., 48, 51, 53, 55, 57, 59, 61, 63, 65, 68, 69
Christian Härtel, Berlin: S. 71
Landesarchiv Berlin: S. 64
Andreas Muhs, Berlin: S. 72, 75
Ullstein Bild, Berlin: Front cover

Front cover: Hollywood stars Mary Pickford and Douglas Fairbanks at a window of the Hotel Adlon, 1926.

Contents

20.000 B.C.
700 A.D.
1237
1320
1417
1539
1685
1786
1806
1848
1871
1914
1918
1929
1933
1939
1945
1953
1961
1973
1987
1989
1990
from 2000 onwards

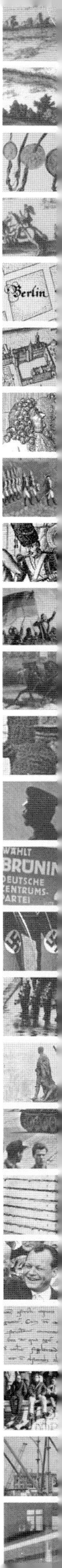

A Unique City

"Everything that happened in Berlin was without comparison",wrote author Carl Sternheim (1878–1942) with a certain irony. "Buildings which had just been erected were continually being torn down to be replaced with better ones, deep into the earth and high into sky. Monuments were demolished by the dozen to make way for greater apotheoses. The population consumed breathlessly, not only to encourage quicker consumption through increased production, but because hysterically spiralling production was the only means of occupying the happily profiteering masses in a time of such rapid growth." When using these words to describe the thriving German capital in the opening decades of the twentieth century, Sternheim could not possibly have imagined the extent of the destruction and amazing new building both "into the earth and the sky" that would follow. What were once the little medieval twin towns of Berlin/Cölln became the Hohenzollern seat of power and later the Prussian capital, but it was only after the founding of the German Empire in 1871 that the city received the real push of development that enabled it to grow into a true metropolis. The images, myths and clichés associated with this era continue to influence our idea of Berlin to this day. Perhaps the most lasting impressions were those made by the Twenties, which were characterized on the one hand by deep political strife and on the other by a highly productive cultural life, although the most radical reorganization of the city and its inhabitants occurred under the National Socialists. They drew up plans to construct their world city of "Germania" in Berlin, forced tens of thousands of Berliners into exile, indeed even to their deaths, and left behind a city in ruins. Yet to many foreign visitors Berlin remains the city of the Wall, that most absurd construction in history which gave a concrete form to the division of the world into West and East. When the Iron Curtain fell in November 1989 it was also in Berlin that the Cold War came to a peaceful end. The people danced on top of the Wall at the Brandenburg Gate and soon began to dismantle the "Anti-fascist Protection Wall" with hammers and chisels.

Berlin's most defining quality is its ability to keep changing. It has always retained something provisional about it, including the waste-land and problems with transport links which resulted from war damage and the years of division. Even if in the 1990s construction work was started to heal these wounds in the city landscape and whole new districts, such as the area around Postdamer Platz, have been created , there will always be corners of the city where something new is emerging and where there are new discoveries to be made. In the final analysis this is what makes Berlin such a fascinating city for both its visitors and its people.

Colonia on the Spree

The Medieval twin towns

Slav rule and the conversion to Christianity

The glacial valley in which Berlin, according to its inhabitants “came to lie”, was formed after the last Ice Age 20,000 years ago by the snow and ice melting from the glaciers. The valley more or less follows the course of the river Spree, bordered by the Barnim plain in the north and the Teltow plain in the south.

In contrast with later centuries, in its early history the area around Berlin was extremely sparsely populated. After the number of inhabitants was greatly reduced by the great migration of peoples in the 4th Century A.D., the area was practically depopulated by the middle of the 6th Century. The Germanic tribes who had settled here over a period of several centuries left little more than the names of the two rivers, the Spree and the Havel to their successors, the Slavs. Two tribes ruled the region: the “Heveller” in the west with Brandenburg as their main settlement and seat of power and the “Sprewaner” in the east, whose main town was Köpenick. The two areas were separated by a band of forest which encompassed the natural crossing point of the Spree in the glacial valley and where later the twin towns of Berlin/Cölln would grow up. The remnants of this green no man’s land still exist today as the Tegeler Forst and the Grunewald.

But first, one of the most important settlements in the Berlin area developed further west, where the Spree joins the Havel. This could be the reason that to this day the inhabitants of Spandau look down on their neighbouring “upstarts” from Berlin; their first castle dates back to the year 700 A.D. With its convenient location Spandau soon developed into an early urban centre of great importance. To the east of the same area, in Sprewaner territory, Köpenick developed into an important settlement. There had been a castle complex dating back to about 700 A.D. on an island in the Dahme and in the surrounding area there was a similar, if modest, upturn in economic activity. The region around the Spree crossing point served both tribes mainly as a hunting ground and today the most common explanation of the origin of the name Berlin derives from the Slav root “brl” which denotes a marsh or morass.

The region between the Elbe and the Oder, which also includes Berlin, was ruled mainly by Slav tribes until well into the 10th Century. Ottonian rulers, however, made continued attempts to extend their territory in an easterly direction. Around the middle of the 10th Century Otto I brought all the Slav tribes under the jurisdiction of the German Empire. He set up two Marches (borderlands) to protect his territory; these were later divided and the North March was created in the area around Brandenburg. But then the Slav uprising of 983 A.D. ended the Christianization and expansionism of the German Electors and the Slav inhabitants managed to assure their independence for about 200 years.

First reference to the town of Cölln in a document from the year 1237.

The Ascent of the Askanians

Renewed efforts to expand the Empire were created by the economic upswing after the turn of the first millennium. The regions to the east of the Elbe were brought into the plan again, especially as at the beginning of the 12th Century the Heveller rulers in power in Brandenburg were weakened. In 1134 the German Emperor, Lothar III, appointed the Askanian Prince, Albrecht the Bear, Count of the North March (Graf der Nordmark). An important factor in Albrecht's advancement was his good relations with the Heveller ruler, Pribislaw-Heinrich, who had converted to Christianity. The childless Prince of Brandenburg named Albrecht the Bear as his successor and Albrecht was able to claim his title as early as 1150. His position was threatened, however, by the occupation of Brandenburg by Jaxa, who was probably the Sprewaner ruler of Köpenick. It wasn't until 1157 that Albrecht was able to gain back Brandenburg and from then onwards Albrecht and his successors called themselves the Margraves of Brandenburg. Their principality still consisted of various areas which were not connected to each other. At first the Askanians had to share their dominion of the North March with other German and Slav rulers, but up to the end of the 13th Century they managed through clever politics to keep

1237

Seal of Berlin/Cölln from 1253.

extending their power base. At this point they were ruling over what had become one of the largest German princedoms.

Part of their political plan was the methodical settlement of the March, combined with the founding of towns and monasteries. In the wake of this expansion of their territory two small market towns posts grew up at the crossing point of the Spree, the future towns of Berlin and Cölln.

From the very start the population of Berlin and Cölln consisted mainly of immigrants, with only few Slavs from the immediate surroundings among them. Newcomers came from the area around Quedlingburg, Ballenstedt and Aschersleben where the Askanians had their ancestral seats, as well as a group from the Rhineland. This could explain the highly plausible derivation of the name Cölln/Colonia from Köln on the Rhein. The settlement of the Teltow and the Barnim plains later made the crossing point of the Spree into a route junction.

The first references to both Berlin and Cölln were made in written sources dating back to 1237 or 1244, which officially document the beginning of their urban development. In a contract from the year 1237, made between Bishop Gernand of Brandenburg and the Margraves Johann I and Otto III, a Reverend Symeon of Cölln was named as witness.

First and foremost the Margraves used the twin towns to secure the crossing point of the Spree and they served as a settlement for craftsmen and weavers. Although the Margraves set up a regional court in Berlin/Cölln in the second half of the 13th Century, they stayed mostly in Spandau castle. Economic progress was promoted by the trading law forcing travelling merchants to offer their wares for a certain period to the inhabitants of the town and for a long time the most significant imports were Flanders cloth and salt-water fish. Berlin/Cölln thus partly developed into a fish market of great

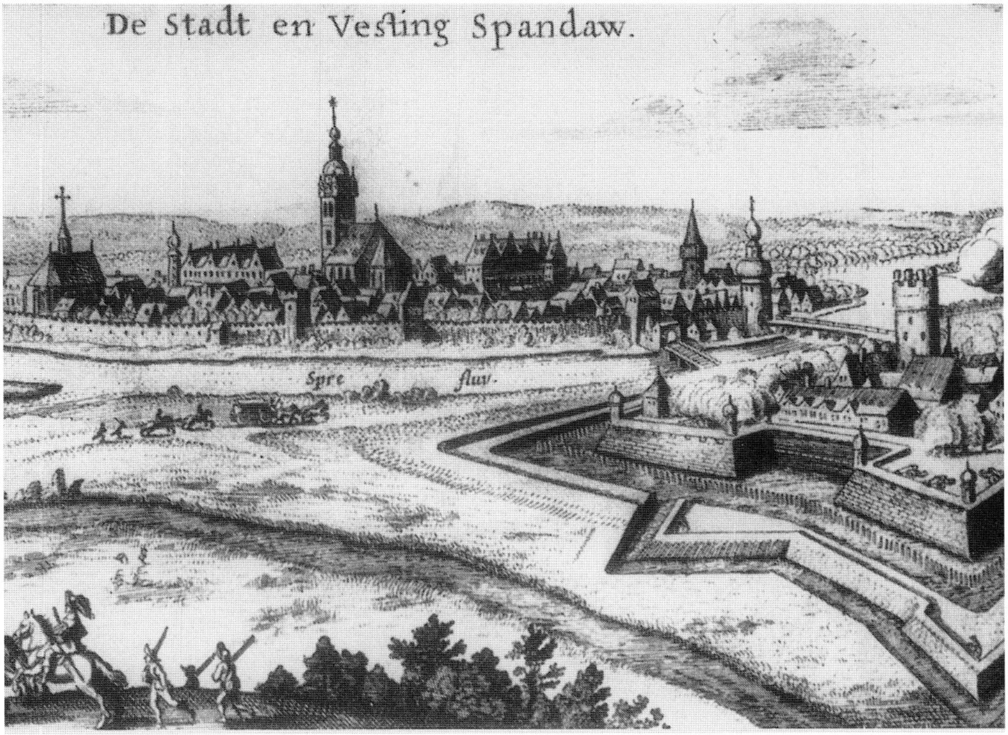

The town and fortress of Spandau in an engraving from the mid-17th century.

importance where most of the local fish was also sold.

Towards the end of the 13th Century the twin towns had outstripped the nearby older towns of Köpenick and Spandau in importance and in 1280 the first Parliament of the Mark of Brandenburg was set up in Berlin /Cölln. The nobility from the Prignitz and the Mid- and Old March all gathered here, a clear sign that the twin towns had already become the Capital of the Mark of Brandenburg.

The end of Askanian rule came with the death of the childless Askanians, Waldemar and Heinrich in 1319 and 1320. There then followed a time of a shifting balance of power during which the Wittelsbachers and Luxemburgers struggled for influence in the region and the twin towns were able to further extend their privileges. The urban settlements on either side of the Spree pursued a policy of co-operation, committed themselves to mutual aid and formed a joint Council which existed alongside the Councils of the individual towns. The Town Hall where they met up stood on the Long Bridge which linked the two halves of the town: in more recent times, therefore, Berlin was able to refer to a wealth of experience of being a divided town centuries ago.

Merchants, Electors and Kings

From the Thirty Years War to Frederick the Great

1417
1539

The rule of the Hohenzollern

Political stability did not return to the town until Friedrich I of Hohenzollern (1371–1440) was proclaimed Margrave and Elector on 17th April 1417. With the Hohenzollern, a noble family had arrived on the scene who were to play a central role in shaping the destiny of the city until the year 1918.

From the 15th Century onwards the townscape was clearly determined by building work undertaken by the Princes, even if until 1486 the Mark of Brandenburg was seen more as an offshoot of their Frankonian possessions around Ansbach and Kulmbach. The Margrave claimed a large piece of land for himself near Cölln on which to build his royal seat. However, at first he was not made at all welcome and his attempt to appropriate large chunks of his citizens' land met with open resistance. Showing the indignation for which Berliners are well known, the locals staged an uprising to fight against their subjugation to princely rule and initially managed to prevent the building of the palace. It wasn't until the spring of 1451 that the Margrave was able to move into his new residence.

It has to be said that nothing of much significance emerged from the Berlin seat of power. Even amongst the towns of the Mark of Brandenburg Berlin was not the leading light. Franfurt an der Oder, for example, was still the more important economic centre until the end of the 16th Century. On the other hand the inhabitants of Berlin were known even then for a healthy sense of self-confidence. After Martin Luther had unleashed the Reformation in the German provinces with his Theses in Wittenberg, the Electors at first remained allied to the Catholic faith. In 1539 the Councils of Berlin and Cölln finally met and demanded from their rulers the introduction of Holy Communion according to the Evangelical rite, which Joachim II (1505–1571) finally granted.

Several important buildings were erected during Joachim's rule. He had the Stadtschloss (City Palace) extended by Caspar Theiss, who had also built the hunting palaces in the Grunewald and at Köpenick. In addition he was responsible for constructing a fast connecting route from his palace to the Grunewald, which led across marshy areas and therefore had to be constructed as a boarded causeway; the Kurfürstendamm (Elector's Causeway).

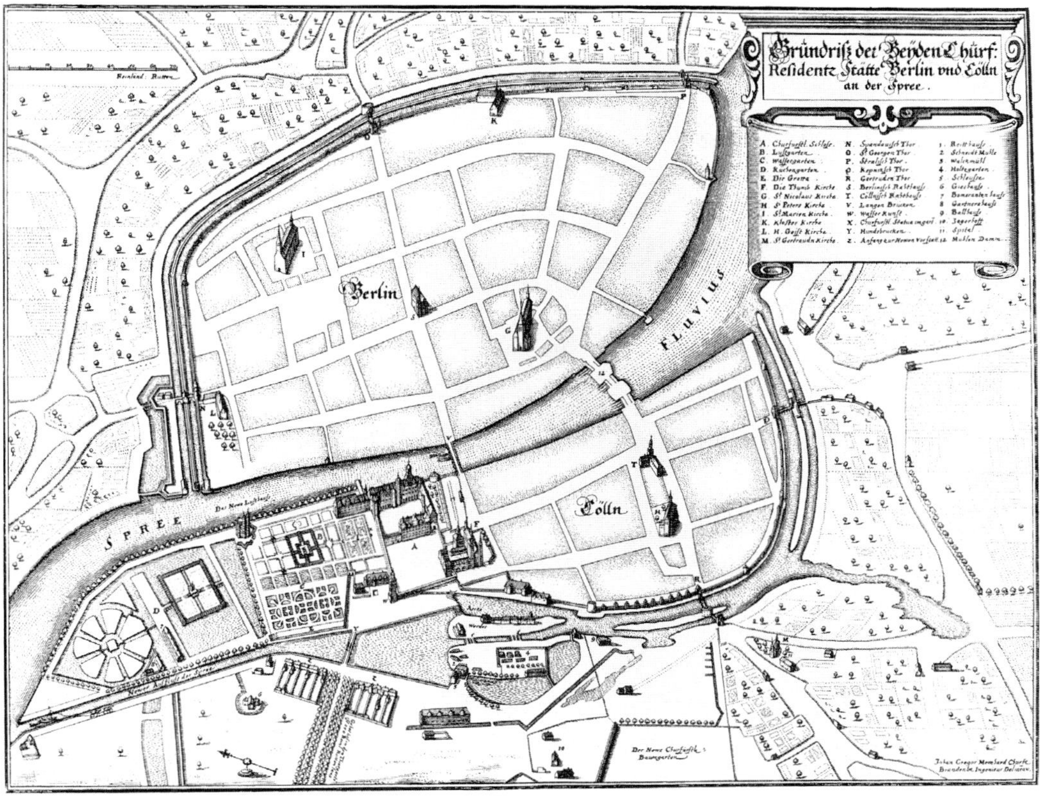

The oldest plan of the twin towns from the year 1650, showing the approximate outline of the medieval layout.

In the second half of the 16th Century the population of the twin towns had reached an estimated 12,000. When compared with the European capitals such as London and Paris, which at this time could already count their inhabitants in hundreds of thousands, it is easy to understand why Berlin can only be described in those days as a young city growing up in a provincial backwater. In fact things were only to get worse. The Thirty Years War, which from 1618 to 1648 turned the whole of Europe into a battlefield, did not leave the Mark of Brandenburg untouched. At least Berlin was spared any direct action during the initial years of the war but then later it fell victim to Imperial pillaging when the Hohenzollerns allied themselves with the Swedish King, Gustav Adolf II. By the end of the war the town is supposed to have lost a third of its citizens, including many who died in a rampant outbreak of the plague in 1631. The Mark of Brandenburg was among the most devastated parts of the Empire; whole areas were left depopulated and deserted.

The “Great Elector” *(Grosser Kurfürst)*

After the war Friedrich Wilhelm (1620–1688), who went down in history as the Great Elector, made decisions that had a

The Great Elector with Huguenot merchants. Etching by Daniel Chodowiecki, 1786.

1685

profound influence on Berlin's future development. He had the palace further extended, had fortifications constructed in the sixties and strengthened the local garrison to 2,000 men. At the same time private building activity was also stimulated. New building regulations stipulated that the roads had to be cobbled. Lanterns had to be put up and pig sties were no longer permitted on the roads. Construction initiatives were financed by raising a new import tax the "Akzise". New districts developed: Friedrichswerder in the west and Dorotheenstadt to the north of it, as well as various suburbs outside the city wall such as the Spandauer Vorstadt and the Stralauer Vorstadt. By the end of the Great Elector's reign the total area of Berlin had almost doubled in four decades.

However the Mark of Brandenburg could not call on sufficient workers and employers to render his economic policy successful and the Great Elector decided that immigration was the answer. In 1671 the first sizeable group to be assimilated into the Mark were exiled Jews from Vienna. The Edict of Potsdam in 1685 facilitated the immigration of 20,000 Huguenots, who mainly settled in Berlin. The majority of the Huguenots, Protestant refugees from France, set themselves up in business and trade and the Jews in finance and credit. Thus the idea of tolerance, which was to become one of the pillars of the Prussian conception of a state, had its roots in entirely pragmatic considerations.

Prussia becomes a Great Power

The son of the Great Elector, Friedrich I (1657–1713) finally took the royal crown for the Hollenzollern by having himself crowned King in Prussia in 1701. During his reign both state and city flourished culturally. In 1694 he called the architect, Andreas Schlüter to Berlin to begin on alterations to the Palace and undertake the works on the Zeughaus (Arsenal). Together with other architects such as Eosander von Göthe, Schlüter brought a new elegance to the royal capital both with these projects and others on various private residences.

Sophie Charlotte (1668–1705), Queen of Prussia, also played a large part in stimulating academic life and culture. She was responsible for bringing the philosopher and mathematician Gottfried Wilhelm Leibniz (1646–1716) to Berlin and on his initiative the Electoral Brandenburg Society of Sciences, later the Academy of Sciences, was founded.

The double existence of Berlin/Cölln came to an end on the eighth anniversary of Friedrich's coronation. Together with their suburbs of Friedrichswerder, Dorotheenstadt and Friedrichsstadt, they were amalgamated into one administrative unit which became the centre of the monarchy. The unified community of Berlin had come into being and by the end of Friedrich I's rule the population of Berlin was 60,000.

His successor to the throne, Friedrich Wilhelm I, was soon given the nickname "The Soldier King". He reformed the state household, cared nothing for his father's great love of splendour and stood for rationality and sobriety. Instead of investing in prestige and image he increased the size of the standing army to 80,000 men. This strengthening of the military was intended to get Berlin finally on a par with other European capitals, but it also stimulated the city's economic development and the manufacture of rifles and textiles flourished. One of the benefactors of this development was the rifle factory Splitgerber & Daum, founded in 1712. The Berlin garrison was also steadily growing; in 1720 there were about 12,000 soldiers and their families living in the city. The economic growth attracted more and more new citizens to the region, among them for example the Bohemian Protestants. They mainly settled in the surrounding countryside, in Böhmisch-Rixdorf or Neu-Schöneberg. Berlin was now slowly developing into a European city, both in population and in area. The old fortifications had become a hindrance to new building schemes and they were razed to the ground in the 1730s. The sites of the former city gates were turned into squares with striking features such as the round tower at the Hallesches Tor (now Mehringplatz), the octagon at Potsdamer Platz (Leipziger Platz), and the Quarré at the Brandenburg Gate (Pariser Platz), which to this day are an important part of Berlin's architectural heritage. From 1738 onwards a six metre high customs wall, the "Akzisemauer", was built.

The first Potsdamer Tor. Engraving from the year 1780.

This wall encircled a larger area of the city than the previous fortifications and was intended to prevent smuggling and desertion, but no longer had any significance as a fortification. Reconstructed remains can still be seen today on the middle stretch of Stresemannstrasse in Kreuzberg.

Berlin under Friedrich II

"Religions must all be tolerated and the state must just be vigilant that no-one does anyone harm because here everyone must allowed to be spiritual after their own fashion." This famous remark by Friedrich II (1712–1786), son of the Soldier King, is a good example of the long tradition of the Prussian concept of tolerance.

Through numerous drawn-out wars, such as the Seven Year War against the Habsburgs for the Province of Silesia, Friedrich II turned Prussia into a power of European significance. But above all, successive generations saw in Frederick the Great (Friedrich der Grosse)

Friedrich II, King of Prussia.

a symbolic figure embodying all the virtues required of a Prussian; an appreciation of culture, a sense of duty and military might.

With the King's support Berlin developed into an intellectual centre on the European model. From 1750 until 1753 Voltaire, the French philosopher of the Enlightenment, lived at the court in Potsdam where the King preferred to spend his time and where he had his favourite palace of Sanssouci built. It was this kind of intellectual milieu that attracted citizens interested in science and literature, especially Jews, to Berlin. They gathered around the publisher Friedrich Nicolai, the philosopher Moses Mendelssohn or the writer Gotthold Ephraim Lessing and with the relaxation of censorship the publication of new journals could go ahead. In 1740 alongside the "Vossische Zeitung" which had first appeared in 1721 under the name of the "Berlinische Priviligierte Zeitung", the second largest newspaper came into being, the "Berlinische Nachrichten von Staats- und Gelehrtensachen".

Friedrich II also left behind an architectural landscape whose traces are clearly visible today. The central feature was the Forum Fridericianum which the King planned together with the architect Georg Wenzeslaus von Knobelsdorff (1699–1753). The first building to be erected was the Staatsoper (State Opera House) on Unter den Linden, which is still standing today. Then followed the St.Hedwigskathedrale, the Prinz-Heinrich-Palais (now the main building of the Humboldt-Universität) and later, from 1775–1780, following G.G. Boumann's plans, the library on Bebelplatz with the nickname"Kommode" (chest of drawers). Unter den Linden became a magnificent boulevard and the Tiergarten (palace hunting grounds) was turned into a landscaped park designed by the landscape gardener Peter Joseph Lenné.

It was during this period that Berlin's theatre history also began. The Französisches Schauspielhaus, which had been opened on the Gendarmenmarkt in 1776, was reopened ten years later as the Deutsches Nationaltheater under the direction of Carl Theophil Doebbelin, the leader of a company of actors. It enjoyed such success that after only a few years the architect Carl Gotthard Langhans was commissioned to create a larger, more prestigious building which was opened in 1802 under the name Schauspielhaus (theatre/concert hall). This was where Friedrich Schiller, among others, staged his plays to great public acclaim and today, in memory of this great writer and poet, a statue of him stands between the two cathedrals on the Gendarmenmarkt.

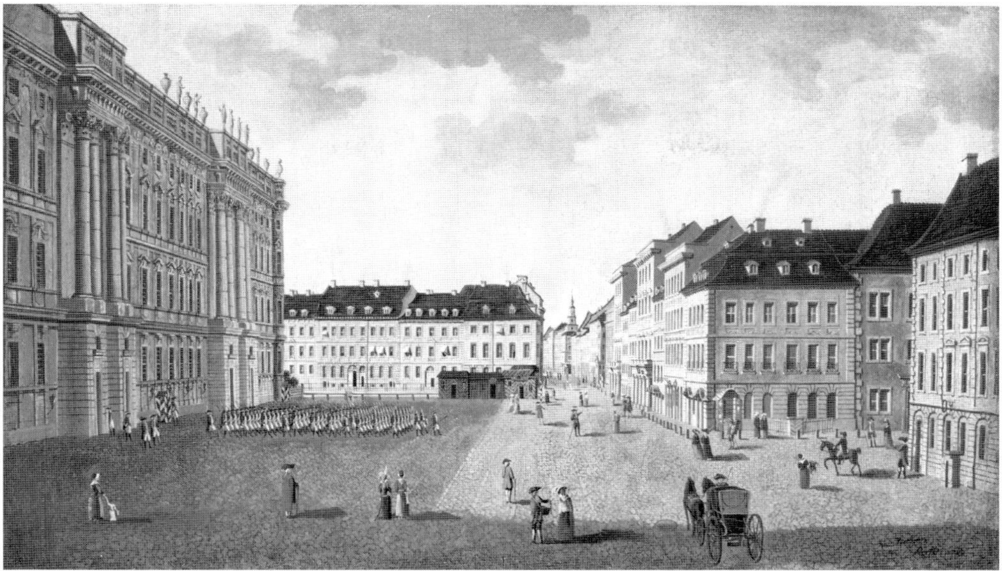

Guards on parade on the Schlossplatz. Painting by Johann Friedrich Fechhelm, 1786.

1786

Another of the King's concerns was the promotion of trade and industry. Goods that could be produced in Prussia were subject to import bans and duty. Coffee beans were heavily taxed in order to support the production of substitutes such as chicory coffee. The state took control of countless manufacturing companies; in 1763 the porcelain manufacturer Gotzkowsky became the renowned KPM (Königlich-Preussische Porzellanmanufaktur).

In 1786, the year of Frederick the Great's death, there were 150,000 people living in Berlin, including numerous soldiers who were billeted on the citizens; barracks were a rare feature of the 18th Century, most of members of the garrison were fully integrated into the life of the city.

Thus in a letter from 1784, the traveller Johann Kaspar Riesbeck wrote: "Berlin is an extremely beautiful and splendid city. It should always be included amongst the most beautiful cities of Europe. It does not possess the uniformity which makes most new and orderly cities boring after a time. The architecture, the planning, the aspect of the public squares, the planting of trees both on the squares and along the streets, in short everything, is full of variety and entertaining."

After the death of Friedrich II Berlin entered a period of upheaval. Under his successor, Friedrich Wilhelm II, heavy censorship rules were re-introduced and state support of the economy was greatly reduced. However, the city has to thank this King for its most significant piece of architecture; the Brandenburg Gate (Brandenburger Tor), handed over to the public in 1791, without any great ceremony. Designed by the architect Carl Gotthard Langhans and adorned with Gottfried Schadow's Quadriga, the "Brandenburg Gate" remains to this day the unequivocal symbol of Berlin.

Berlin becomes a Metropolis

Royal Prussian Capital and Capital of the German Empire

From the Napoleonic Wars to the Wars of Liberation

1806

"The King has lost a battle. Now the first duty of the citizen is peace. I require the inhabitants of Berlin to do their duty. Long live the King and his brothers!" This proclamation on 17th October 1806 by the Governor of Berlin, Duke Friedrich Wilhelm von Schulenburg, was meant to quell panic amongst the population. In the battle near Jena and Auerstedt the Prussian troops had been beaten by Napoleon's forces. This defeat marked the end of Frederick the Great's old Prussia; almost half the land and population were lost and Berlin was occupied by French troops from 1806 until 1808. The occupation began on 27th October 1806 when the French marched through the Brandenburg Gate and Napoleon had the Quadriga removed and taken to Paris as spoils of war. Further confiscation of state property, the billeting of French troops, supplies to the army and maintenance costs for the occupying soldiers created a sizeable burden of debt. Unsurprisingly, resistance to the occupation began to grow. A focal point of the opposition was Georg Reimer's publishing house whose authors included Schleiermacher, Fichte, Arndt, Kleist and the Grimm brothers. Georg Fichte's "Speeches to the German Nation", delivered in the winter of 1807/1808, marked the beginning of a new sense of national identity.

In the end the French occupation resulted in some positive developments and reforms were set in motion whose aim was to revitalise the Prussian State. In overall control was Karl Freiherr (Baron) vom und zum Stein (1757–1831) who acted as Prime Minister. For Berlin the most significant reform was the new urban directive introduced in 1808, which was intended to pave the way for towns and cities to administrate themselves and to involve their citizens in politics. For this purpose a new forum in the shape of a Town Council was introduced, to which councillors were elected by the citizens in free and secret ballots. However, only citizens with an annual income of over 200 Talers were entitled to vote, which at this time was not even seven per cent of the population. Voting rights were therefore still restricted to a small elite circle.

A further important sign of the emergence of a democratic, enlightened society was the foundation in October 1810 of the Friedrich Wilhelms Universität, named after its sponsor. In its first year 52 professors taught just 256 students in the former Prinz Heinrich

French occupation troops march through the Brandenburg Gate.

Palais opposite the State Opera House. The foundation was the idea of Wilhelm von Humboldt, Director of Culture and Education in the Home Office, and it quickly became an early example of state-run academic life. Soon the university attracted an elite group of German academics, among them Fichte, Friedrich Karl von Savigny, the theologian Friedrich Schleiermacher and later the historian Leopold von Ranke and the philosopher Georg Wilhelm Friedrich Hegel.

In this period Luise (1776–1810), Queen of Prussia and wife of Friedrich Wilhelm III, gained considerable popularity with the people. She behaved as a real “First Lady”, kept in close contact with the reformers around von Stein and looked after the concerns of her subjects, who in turn showed her great affection.

When French troops marched in for the second time in March 1812, the Berliners were once more under siege and their city became a centre of the resistance against Napoleon and his control. The defeats which the French army suffered were the starting point for the Wars of Liberation in which a large proportion of the population took up arms in the fight against Napoleon. Out of the 10,000 volunteers from Prussia almost 6,000 came from Berlin. Napoleon’s attempts to take control of the city again failed in August 1813 in the Battle of Großbeeren, south of Berlin. French rule in Germany ended in October of the same year with the Battle of the Nations (Völkerschlacht) near Leipzig.

Restoration and Economic Ascendancy

For a while, however, the hopes of politically progressive forces remained unfulfilled. They had dreamed of a German National State but King Friedrich Wilhelm III did not keep his constitutional promise and instead the citizens experienced a period of restoration with stricter censorship and the persecution of national-liberals.

Prevented from using their energies in the political arena, many citizens pursued cultural or economic goals. If liberal ideas were suppressed in politics they flourished in commercial and economic life. In 1810 the introduction of free trade in Prussia ended the established barriers and had a stimulating effect on Berlin's economic development; by the 1830s industrialisation was in full swing in Prussia and Berlin. The cityscape began to alter radically. Key industries were the textile industry, with cotton printing works, silk manufacturers and production centres for ready-made clothing and those associated with the engineering and metal industries.

Often it was individual entrepreneurs who introduced new industries. In 1837 in North Berlin, in front of the Oranienburger Tor in Chausseestrasse, August Borsig founded a workshop which rapidly rose to become one of the most important engineering factories and subsequently Europe's largest locomotive factory.

The railway soon became the most important driving force in economic development; the demands of increasing traffic could only be met by enlarging the rail network. The first Prussian railway line ran between Berlin and Potsdam and was opened on 29th October 1838. Soon bustling city life developed around Potsdam station and in the 1860s the first blocks of flats were built around Potsdamer Platz. To the south-west of the square the so-called Geheimratsviertel (Privy Council quarter) grew up, an exclusive residential suburb where for a time, the authors Joseph Freiherr (Baron) von Eichendorff and Jacob and Wilhelm Grimm lived. One of the few "original" buildings still standing is the St. Matthäus Kirche, a church designed by Friedrich August Stüler and erected between 1844 and 1846, which today is flanked by the Neue Nationalgalerie and the Gemäldegalerie.

When the Akzisemauer was torn down in 1866, life on Potsdamer Platz and the area to the south of it became increasingly colourful and the buildings more mundane. Potsdamer Strasse developed into a shopping high street and the distinguished inhabitants of the Geheimratsviertel fled to exclusive colonies further out and left their plots of land to speculators. The problems associated with such rapid growth had already started in the 1840s. In 1800 there had been about 170,000 people living in Berlin and by 1849 the population had more than doubled to 412,154. Numerous immigrants had had high hopes of good job opportunities in the city but the growing population had also brought an increase in social problems. The conflicts between the wealthy citizens and the

The Borsig engineering works in Moabit, around 1850.

workers, the wage earners and the small traders intensified.

Contemporaries tried to shake the public with descriptions of the social deprivation in Berlin: "Living in one of the so-called family houses is not much better than being homeless", wrote Friedrich Sass in 1864. "Between 1,600 and 1,800 people live in these five buildings by the Hamburger Tor. They were built at a cost of 80,000 Taler and the owners are now asking 200,000 Talers for them. The rent is 24 Talers per room, which often holds more than one family, and if there is a small dark kitchen area then the rent is 36 Taler. At the moment capital investment is growing at 12 percent."

However it was at this time of lack of political freedom and rising social problems that Berlin flourished both in the arts and sciences. One of the most renowned figures to leave his mark on this era and whose buildings still characterise the city was Karl Friedrich Schinkel (1781–1841). Of all the buildings Schinkel created, the National Memorial to the Wars of Liberation, erected on the highest part of the Tempelhofer Berge, should be mentioned first. The cross at the top of the monument gave the hill its name and during the second half of the 19th Century the city district of Tempelhof was also named after it. Then followed the Neue Wache (The New Guard-house) built

The Schauspielhaus on Gendarmenmarkt, designed by Karl Friedrich Schinkel (above).

between 1816 and 1818 on Unter den Linden between the Zeughaus and the University, the Schauspielhaus on the Gendarmenmarkt, which had a grand opening in 1821 with a production of Goethe's "Iphigenie", as well as the Altes Museum (Old Museum) opposite the Stadtschloss, the first building to be erected on Museumsinsel (Museum Island). In addition Schinkel also designed the Schlossbrücke (Palace Bridge) and the nearby Friedrichswerdersche Kirche and the Bauakademie (Building Academy). The Bauakademie no longer exists of course, but for some time a copy of part of its façade has been erected on the original site.

Alongside this era of great architecture and sculpture, whose most outstanding representatives were Gottfried Schadow and Christian Daniel Rauch, was a very productive and creative phase in the world of opera and theatre. In 1821 Carl Maria von Weber's opera "Freischütz" was premiered at the Schauspielhaus in Berlin. Giacomo Meyerbeer, Felix Mendelssohn-Bartholdy, Albert Lortzing and Carl Friedrich Zelter, the founder of the Acadamy for Singing, were all actively working in Berlin. It is Zelter to whom we owe the rediscovery of J S Bach's music: the performance of the St. Matthew Passion in the Singakademie (now the Maxim Gorki Theatre), conducted by Mendelssohn on 11th March 1829, became a unique musical event.

It was the era of the salons which functioned as centres for the exchange of ideas among great literary, academic and political minds. The most well-known were those run by Rahel Varnhagen and Henriette Herz, which were frequented by personalities such as the Humboldt brothers, Hegel, Adalbert von Chamisso, Heinrich Heine or Achim and Bettina von Arnim.

But of course there were also more mundane pleasures which flourished during this time – and not just for the masses. The Lesekonditoreien (reading cafés) were an especially great attraction. The first of these was opened in 1818 by the Swiss confectioner Giovanoli at 21, Charlottenstrasse. Together with other immigrant proprietors like Stehely, with his café "An der Stechbahn", and "Spargnapani" at 50, Unter den Linden, he was responsible for the rise of the Berlin coffee-house culture. People met up to exchange ideas, but also to see and be seen, just as they did in the salons. In the Lesecafés they could read German and foreign newspapers and learn and talk about current affairs. Certain cafés soon became associated with particular political leanings: the Liberals and Radicals met at Stehely's, the Conservatives at Café Josty. In the troubled times before 1848 Karl Marx, Friedrich Engels, Michael Bakunin and Max Stirner were regular customers in Stehely's and by contrast the Guards Officers and big landowners met at the Hofkonditorei Kranzler on Unter den Linden. From 1833 onwards Kranzler owned and ran Berlin's first pavement café.

The less well-off went to less sophisticated places for their entertainment, many of which were to be found by the city gates, for example the Bötzow brewery on Windmühlenberg (Windmill Hill) in the present-day Prenzlauer Berg district or the Hasenheide where there were numerous Gartenlokale (garden pubs). The Tiergarten to the west of the Brandenburg Gate had also become an area for relaxation and leisure. Here there were Zelten-Lokale (pubs in tents) which were used both for pleasure and for meetings.

Rahel Varnhagen von Ense, engraving from 1817.

The name "In den Zelten" (in the tents) derived from the temporary nature of the summer pubs which had to be dismantled again during the winter months.

Revolutionary Berlin

Berliners in the "Lesecafés" and in "In den Zelten" began to voice their dissatisfaction with the political situation in Prussia. When Friedrich Wilhelm IV took over power in 1840 they had had high expectations of reforms, but nothing happened and news of the Silesian weavers' uprising in 1844 made many Berliners aware of their own miserable social plight. The first warning signal for the authorities came during the same year when the former Mayor of Storkow, Heinrich Ludwig Tschech attempted to assassinate the King and his wife. A little verse started going round Berlin:

"Aber keiner war so frech,/ Wie der Bürgermeister Tschech,/ Denn er traf fast auf ein Haar/ Unser teures Königspaar./Ja, er traf die Landesmutter/ Durch den Rock ins Unterfutter." (Loosely translated: There was once a cheeky mayor, who nearly killed our royal pair. Yes, he even got the Prussian mare, right through her skirt to her underwear!)

1848

Price increases and poor harvests caused unrest and looting on the city streets. On the Gendarmenmarkt the enraged mass even stormed the market stands and the army had to be brought in to stem this uprising, which has gone down in history as the Potato Revolution. Finally, the atmosphere was so charged that it would have taken very little to turn things into something much bigger. At the beginning of 1848, meetings were held all over the city where people could voice their dissatisfaction with social conditions. Citizens and workers met again during the first few days of March to discuss their grievances. On 17th March they decided to hand the King a list of demands which included guaranteeing the freedom of the press, summoning the Landtag (Regional Parliament) and deploying a militia. The King actually appeared quite willing to give into some of the demands, but on 18th March unrest and panic set in after two shots were fired at the masses in front of the palace. Barricades were erected against the King's soldiers and over 200 people were killed in the street riots that followed.

At noon on 19th March the army at last received the order to withdraw. The King honoured the dead as they lay in state in front of the Schlosspalast and allowed the citizens to raise a militia and granted freedom of assembly as well as freedom of the press. It all looked as if the revolution had been victorious.

On 1st May the elections began for the Prussian National Assembly which met for the first time on 22nd May. However there was further unrest. Finally, on 14th June, the Zeughaus was stormed by demonstrators who demanded that the people should be systematically armed. Slowly public opinion began to change in the face of such events; people were afraid of complete disorder. As a result the King ordered his troops to march into the city again under the pretext: "Berlin needs to be tamed." The freedom of the press was repealed and the militia were dissolved. On 5th December a constitution was drawn up which made Prussia a constitutional monarchy. At first it even enshrined the universal and equal right to vote, but by 30th May 1849 this had been replaced by the "three tier vote", which favoured the wealthy middle-classes and the land-owning aristocracy survived in essence until 1918.

The road towards becoming a modern city

Similar inequality ensued in the democratic elections for the City Council; the right to vote required an annual income of 300 Taler and therefore only five per cent of the population could participate. However, it was neither the City Councillors, who were all supporters of the Conservative Party, nor the Lord Mayor who had any real power, but rather the Chief of Police, Carl Ludwig

Fighting at the barricades on Alexanderplatz during the night of 18/19th March 1848.

Friedrich von Hinckeldey. On the one hand he was responsible for controlling and monitoring the population and seeing that "democratic machinations" were nipped in the bud and on the other hand he was in charge of modernising the city's infrastructure. He ordered the regular cleaning of the gutters, had the first water pipes built and a waterworks erected by the Stralauer Tor. Until then, the Berliners had been supplied with fresh water by over 900 public and several thousand private fountains and hand-pumps. The waterworks of "The Berlin Waterworks Company" started operating in 1856 and the city gasworks also initially looked to England for its technology and know-how. The professional fire brigade founded by von Hinckeldey was seen as exemplary and progressive, even when compared with those abroad. At the same time other Berliners also demonstrated their entrepreneurial spirit. Ernst Litfass (1816–1874), owner of a printing works, signed a contract with the Chief of Police, which allowed him to put his advertisement pillars up in the city. These Litfaß pillars stemmed the flow of indiscriminate bill-sticking and by 1868 there were 200 of them in Berlin.

But von Hinckeldey's most enduring legacy, the result of his 1853 building regulation, was probably the tenement houses (Mietskasernen) with several courtyards

The „Building Fever of the Gründerjahre", painting by Friedrich Kaiser.

(Hinterhöfe) which are so typical of Berlin. His regulation required the courtyards to be large enough for a firehose to turn, which meant a length and breadth of exactly 5.34 metres. It was common to find three or four such courtyards one after another, surrounded by buildings to the side and at right angles (often euphemistically referred to as the "Garden House"). This type of building development could be considered as a fatal mistake, but it was the only way to keep up with the rapid increase in population. From1857 to 1871 the population doubled again to over 800,000 inhabitants. The growing city was a magnet for immigrants from the surrounding provinces who came hoping to find work. Numerous speculators doubtless got rich very quickly by accommodating as many tenants as possible in as little space as possible.

Inner city transport also had to adjust to the new conditions and the Berliners' increasing need for mobility. In March 1865 a license was granted for the first horse-drawn railway between Charlottenburg and the Kupfergraben; since the 1840s various horse-drawn buses had been operating all over Berlin. The city's growing self-confidence was reflected in the construction of new Town Hall to replace the medieval one. The Rotes

View of Spandauer Strasse, photograph from 1856.

Ernst Litfass with one of his advertisement pillars.

Rathaus (Red Town Hall), built between 1861 and 1869 and designed by Hermann Friedrich Waesemann, was so-called because of its red brick façade.

The building development plan for Berlin (1859–1861) drawn up by the head of the planning department and building control office, James Friedrich Ludolf Hobrecht (1815–1902), set the course for all future development, although it came in for some heavy criticism when it was first published. It has to be said that the generous road plans have certainly proved their worth – they are even capable of dealing with the stream of 21st Century traffic.

Industrial Expansion in the Imperial Capital (*Die Gründerjahre*)

There was already a feeling that Berlin was turning into a cosmopolitan city during the building boom in the second half of the 19th Century and its incredible growth, within just a few decades, was echoed in contemporary literature. In his novel "Cécile", Theodor Fontane (1818–1898), a witness and chronicler of this phenomenon, had Gordon, one of his heroes, trying in vain to get across Potsdamer Platz, "which was today once

The Reichstag building on Königsplatz.

The entrance gate to the Borsig works in Tegel.

1871

again a futile task because of all the sewerage construction works and the island platform being installed in the middle of it. So Gordon had to try his luck around the periphery and this of course was fraught with new difficulties." Fontane himself lived near the square at 134, Potsdamer Strasse (where the massive new State Library building now stands) and could follow and comment on them at close quarters on the birth pangs of the new Berlin.

Fontane's observations were always accompanied by reminiscences on the old Prussia, which was now more or less in its death throes. Berlin was on the way to becoming the capital of Imperial Germany. The Prussian Prime Minister, Otto Fürst von Bismarck (1815–1898) (Otto, Prince of Bismarck) had already achieved the unification of Germany north of the river Maine by founding the North German Federation in 1866/1867. A Prussian-led amalgamation with the South German States could not proceed because of opposition from Germany's neighbours, France. But Bismarck knew how to turn diplomatic quarrels with France to his political advantage and on 19th July 1870, Prussia declared war on France, using the alliance with the South German States as one of the reasons. When Prussia was victorious, the German Empire was proclaimed on 18th January 1871 from the Hall of Mirrors in the Palace of Versailles. Thus national unity came from above, from the ruling classes and not as the result of a democratic process, as many had hoped. In the peace treaty ratified later, France was forced to give up Alsace-Lothringen and to pay war reparations. This money flowing into the German coffers played a significant part in contributing towards the economic upturn which accompanied the years of industrial expansion.

At first the German Parliament ("Reichstag") was housed in Leipziger Strasse in the former Royal Porcelain Manufacture's building, before the new Reichstag building, designed by Paul Wallot, was built on Königsplatz from 1884–1894.

During this period, important decisions were made in local government politics which paved the way towards a modern city. The most important of these was the

The crossroads at Unter den Linden and Friedrichstrasse in a photo montage from 1900.

construction of the sewers. At the time when Berlin became Imperial capital it still had a very poor sewerage system. Most of the waste flowed untreated through the so-called gutters which ran between the path and the carriageway into the rivers and canals. More importantly the introduction of running water had increased the amount of effluents to such an extent that the gutter capacity would no longer suffice. The new ultra-modern sewerage system installed in Berlin in 1873 was designed by James Hobrecht and sponsored by Rudolf Virchow (1821–1920), a doctor and local politician. After the effluents had been pumped through special pressurised pipes into the surrounding countryside and then distributed on to sewage farms bought up by the city, they served as fertiliser for the land being used for agricultural purposes. The water was then automatically filtered and returned to the water circulation system. This process gave Berlin the reputation of being one of the cleanest cities in the world at the turn of the 20th Century.

This development was accompanied by a further increase in the population of Berlin, or in this case, Greater Berlin, because meanwhile even neighbouring towns like Neukölln (until 1912 Rixdorf) or Wilmersdorf had grown in to cities of over 100,000 inhabitants. At the founding of the German Empire there were about 930,000 people living in Berlin and by 1910 this figure had already reached 3.7 million.

Newly established companies and other economic enterprises attracted more and more

Underground railway construction between Wittenbergplatz and Zoologischer Garten.

people looking for work and wages. The most exciting developments were in the electricity industry, still in its infancy. The first signs of the electrification of Berlin came in 1878 were when Siemens & Halske put up electric lighting in Königstrasse and unveiled a small electric locomotive. AEG (Allgemeine Elektrizitäts-Gesellschaft - General Electric Company) was founded shortly after this and in 1895 a third of all Germans employed in the electricity industry worked in Berlin.

Baroness Spitzemberg recalled the atmosphere in Berlin at this time in her memoirs: "The hurly-burly in the main high streets such as Leipzigerstrasse and Friedrichstrasse is simply bewitching; the electric vehicles and trams form an unbroken line. Vehicles of every kind, carriages, two and three-wheelers in their hundreds run along beside each other, behind and in front of each other and often into each other. The ringing and clinging and the clattering of wheels is ear-splitting; crossing the street is a work of art for the city-dweller and agony for provincial people. Frau von Beulwitz even said that to begin with they had hugged each other when they managed to cross Potsdamer Platz to the island in the middle in one piece! At Wertheim's it is as bustling as a bee-hive and in the bookshops people are fighting each other for a copy of Bismarck's memoirs."

For two decades since 1865 the most important method of transport in the city centre and the suburbs had actually been the horse drawn trains which had only gradually been replaced by newer technology. The first electric tram line ran in 1881 from Lichterfelde East station to the Kadettenanstalt (Officer Cadet Academy). The role of the railway for inner city transport became increasingly important once the circle line came into operation. 1871 saw the inauguration of the east section and the west section was opened six years later. This meant that the various main stations were connected with each other on a direct route. The construction of the urban section between Charlottenburg and Schlesischer station (now Ostbahnhof) right through the city centre took somewhat longer and wasn't completed until 1882. In 1902 the first elevated and underground railway was opened. It ran from Stralauer Tor (the station was later called Osthafen and no longer exists) to Zoologischer Garten with a branch line to Potsdamer Platz and meant that after London, Budapest, Glasgow and Paris, Berlin was the fifth European city to have an underground railway system.

Café Kranzler at 25, Unter den Linden, Photograph from 1912.

Berlin also played a leading role in the field of new methods of transport. After the flight pioneer Otto Lilienthal had carried out the first attempts at gliding in Lichterfelde in 1891, the city soon developed into a centre for air travel. The first airport in Germany, one of the most modern in Europe, was in Johannisthal and it was from here that in August 1912 participants in the "Race around Berlin" took off on their flight over Schulzendorf, Spandau, Potsdam and Teltow.

The first private car was registered in Berlin in 1892 and only a few years later the first motorcar and motorbike races took place. In 1913 the Automobil-, Verkehrs- und Übungsstrassen GmbH constructed a road through the Grunewald which was a forerunner of the motorway. This stretch, best known even today as the AVUS, wasn't actually opened until 1921 and was regularly used as a race-track. What appealed to the individual soon became the most popular form of public transport and buses and carriages with engines rapidly replaced the horse drawn varieties – the last bus of this type was withdrawn from service in 1920.

Echoes of Baroness Spitzemberg's memoirs were of course very much part and parcel of this period between the founding of the Empire and the outbreak of the First World War. There was a flood of companies producing food and consumer goods or dealing in trade, some of whose names are still on the Berlin scene today – the Bolle dairy, Kaiser's coffee shop, Butter-Beck, the textile firms of Leineweber and Peek & Cloppenburg or Tack and Leiser in the shoe trade. Wertheim's department store was established in 1904 in Leipzigerstrasse in a building designed by Alfred Messel which set new standards. In 1907 KaDeWe (Kaufhaus des Westens) opened in Tauentzienstrasse in Charlottenburg and became the symbol and the sponsor of flourishing trade in the Kurfürstendamm and surrounding area at the turn of the century.

It was here that the "city stroller" (der Flaneur) was born. One of the most important representatives of this breed, Franz Hessel (1880–1941) wrote the following: "The Tauentzienstrasse and the Kurfürstendamm have the important cultural mission of teaching the Berliner how to stroll around the city, if this activity is going to take off here. But perhaps its not yet too late. City-strolling is like reading the street, where peoples' faces, displays, shop windows, pavement cafés, rails, cars and trees turn into letters which make up the words, sentences and pages of an ever-changing book. A proper city stroll has no particular purpose and because there is so much on offer in the way of entertainment, food, drink, theatre, film or cabaret between Wittenbergplatz and Halensee, one can set out for a walk with no real aim and just allow the adventure to happen."

With the move to the west, a second important centre came into being alongside the prestigious old Berlin around Unter den Linden and Friedrichstrasse. Part of this change in emphasis was due to the impressive villas and attractive residential estates which had been built, particularly to the west and the south of the city. Here in leafy suburbs such as Lichterfelde, Lankwitz and Grunewald, the rich and well-to-do could live in comfort away from the city crowds.

In art and literature Berlin found it difficult to become a proper capital city. For a long time Adolph Menzel (1815–1905) was the only artist able to make his name as a Realist. Wilhelm von Bode, the Director of the Royal Museums, tried hard to promote the arts in Berlin and in 1898, in protest against the establishment, the Berliner Secession was formed, attracting famous artists such as Max Liebermann and Walter Leistikow.

The German Theatre was founded in 1883 and here Otto Brahm (1894–1903) and Max Reinhardt (1905–1932) set new trends. The People's Theatre Movement was set up to make theatre accessible to less well-off Berliners and in 1911 the premiere of Gerhart Hauptmann's play, "Die Weber" (The Weavers) at the Freie Volksbühne caused a furore.

Berlin became increasingly important in the academic world and in the centenary year of the Friedrich Wilhelms Universität the Kaiser-Wilhelm-Gesellschaft (Emperor William Society) was founded to promote academic research. Max Planck and Albert Einstein, both Nobel Prizewinners, were among its most famous scientists.

Berlin was the undisputed newspaper capital of Germany and in 1880 new names, such as the "Berliner Lokalanzeiger" and the "Berliner Morgenpost", appeared alongside traditional newspapers like the conservative "Kreuz-Zeitung" or the "Vossische Zeitung" and in 1904 the first issue of the "BZ am Mittag" was published.

However, developments in world politics were soon to interrupt Berlin's peaceful development into one of the most modern

Crowds watching the return of the Kaiser's defeated troops as they come through the Brandenburg Gate on 10th December 1918.

cities in Europe. In striving to become one of the most important Imperial powers in Europe, the German government had become too confrontational. When the Austrian heir to the throne was assassinated in Sarajewo in 1914 the German Empire, as an ally of Austro-Hungary, went to war against the great European powers of Russia, Italy, France and England.

Even though the First World War was not fought on German soil, its effects still had consequences for life in the capital. Berlin became the centre of war planning and production which involved firms such as Siemens and AEG and above all, feeding the population of a large city in conditions of war proved extremely problematic. The authorities set up people's kitchens in each of the Berlin boroughs and in the so-called "Swede winter" of 1917–18, over 150,000 people made use of this provision, although large sections of the population continued to starve. In April 1917, when hopes of an early end to the war and the prospect of victory began to fade, hundreds of thousands of Germans all over the Empire laid down their tools and in October 1918 the figure reached half a million. This protest heralded the end of hostilities but it was also the end of an epoch, which was to be sealed by the November Revolution in 1918.

The Roaring Twenties

Berlin in the Weimar Republic

Insurgent marines in the Berliner Schloss, March 1919.

Volunteer Corps, Revolutionaries, Democrats

On 9th November 1918 the German Chancellor, Prince Max von Baden, made an announcement which marked the end of the Hohenzollern rule, not only over Berlin but over the whole of Germany. "The Emperor and King has decided to renounce the throne. He intends to suggest to his Regent that he should appoint the Member of Parliament, Ebert, as Chancellor and table a bill calling for the general election of a constitutional German National Assembly whose task is to finally settle the future type of state for the German people, including all those peoples of the Empire who want to be included within Germany's borders."

With the end of the monarchy began a time of uncertainty. Would the Social Democratic Party (SPD) take power and lead the country on to the path of parliamentary democracy or would the bands of workers and soldiers who had formed all over the country prove to be stronger? Friedrich Ebert (1871–1925) and the SPD finally managed to set up an election for a constitutional National Assembly on January 19th 1919.

All over Germany there was still political unrest and fighting which was concentrated in Berlin. On 5th January Karl Liebknecht and the USPD (Unabhängige Sozialdemokratische Partei Deutschlands – Independent German Social Democratic Party) called for Ebert's government to be overthrown. The battles that followed were mainly fought by supporters of the Spartacus Group who occupied central points in the city, including the Police Headquarters on Alexanderplatz and the newspaper district around Kochstrasse, Leipzigerstrasse and Friedrichstrasse. The government had to summon the help of the Volunteer Corps (Freikorps) to quell the uprising. The leaders, Karl Liebknecht and Rosa Luxemburg, were arrested and murdered by members of the Cavalry and Rifle Division on the way to Moabit prison. An end to the violence was not in sight.

In the elections for the National Assembly, in which women had the vote for the first time, the SPD, the Centre and the other democratic parties gained a 75 percent majority. On 6th February the Assembly held its inaugural sitting, but for reasons of security it met in Weimar rather than Berlin, in the hope of it passing off without any disturbances. In fact the situation in Berlin remained politically unstable right up to 1920. The government could only maintain power by enlisting the help of counter-revolutionary forces and the final big uprising in Berlin was the right-wing radical Kapp-Putsch from 13th to 17th March 1920. The President Friedrich Ebert and further members of the government and the National Assembly fled from the city, but most state workers refused to work for the leaders of the putsch and eventually a general strike called by the unions forced the subversive elements to surrender.

Greater Berlin between inflation and stabilisation

Democratic reforms in local government had also been pushed through and on 23rd February 1919 a new City Council was elected. The three tier right to vote was abolished and women were also allowed to vote. The SPD and USPD together gained a two-thirds majority and in the Prussian Parliament on 27th April 1920 they jointly passed the "Law on the formation of a new Berlin municipality", which was intended to make lasting changes to the structure and development of the city. The law came into force on 1st October of the same year. The 3.8 million inhabitants, who were distributed amongst Berlin (1.9 million), seven further towns with 1.2 million and 59 country communities, as well as 27 estates, were now under one municipal authority. At the same time Greater Berlin was divided into ten boroughs and covered an area of 878 square kilometres but this did not mean that it was a large "red" Berlin as the middle-class parties had at first feared. In the "old" Berlin the SPD had held the absolute majority of votes but now Greater Berlin included the wealthy residential suburbs which led to more of a political balance. This was partly the reason why the SPD chose Gustav Böss (1873–1946), who was from the middle classes and joined the DDP (Deutsche Demokratische Partei) later in life, as the first long-serving Lord Mayor of Greater Berlin from 1921 until 1930.

1918

Despite signs of political stabilisation, the first years of the Weimar Republic and the new Berlin remained restless. In the Peace Treaty of Versailles in 1919 the victors had made enormous reparation demands on

Germany – a large millstone for a Democracy still its infancy. In particular, right-wing parties and groups tried to denounce the democratic forces as "appeasers" and thereby strengthen their own position. A prominent victim of this agitation was Walther Rathenau, the Foreign Secretary, Head of AEG, formerly responsible for the German war economy, and of Jewish extraction. He was murdered on 24th June 1922 on a public road on the drive from his villa in the Grunewald to the Foreign Office by the terrorist organisation "Consul". Ironically, he had been trying to lessen the burden of reparations and rescue Germany from political isolation.

At the same time the German currency was suffering a series of dramatic crises. Inflation reached its highest point in November 1923 when one American dollar was worth 4.2 billion Marks. The economy began to stabilise in 1924 with the decision to introduce the "rentenmark" on 16th October and the formulation of the Dawes Plan. The symbolic figure for recovery was Gustav Stresemann, (Deutschnationale Volkspartei/DVP German National People's Party) who on August 13th 1923 became German Chancellor for a while and, together with a grand coalition consisting of the DVP, the DDP, the Centre and the SPD, led the country into the so-called stabilisation plan.

A city on the move

There are many pictures that shape our vision of life in Berlin in the twenties. One of them is of a city permanently on the move and when cars became increasingly fashionable, more and more Berliners had their own transport. Potsdamer Platz became a place of perpetual motion. It was less of a square in the classic sense and more of a point where the various streams of city traffic crossed – pedestrians, horse-drawn carriages, cars, buses, trams and underground trains. The traffic tower in the middle of the square became a symbol of the time, a traffic signal which had a normal clock and a look-out for a traffic policeman. The volume of traffic was certainly impressive and for a time Potsdamer Platz was the busiest crossroads in Europe. Some contemporaries, however, could not hide their mockery of the Berliner's attitude towards traffic. Kurt Tucholsky wrote: "It is almost ridiculous what is being erected to organise, to statistically record, to describe, to regulate and to divert the traffic in this city. Is there such a lot of it? No." Tucholsky's observation is borne out by hard facts. In the year 1930 only 49,623 private cars were registered in Berlin.

Ernst Reuter (1889–1953), then City Councillor for Transport, was in favour of merging the numerous companies which were operating public transport. This led to the founding of the Berliner Verkehrs-Gesellschaft (BVG – Berlin Transport Company), which was at that time the largest local government enterprise in the world.

Civilian air traffic was also on the increase, mainly due to the founding of Lufthansa based at Tempelhof Airport, which developed into an international traffic junction during the twenties. In 1924 there were about 1,000 take-offs and landings and four years later this had already increased to an annual figure of 20,800.

Of course the imagination of city planners also took flight during these years. This was particularly true of Potsdamer Platz, the small

Alexanderplatz with the Rotes Rathaus in the background, about 1930.

space into which so many of the historic events of 20th century were compressed. Again and again there were plans to redesign it and in the twenties city planners and architects sought to adapt local conditions to the requirements of a modern city, although many of their ideas never got past the planning stage. One is reminded of the design by the Luckhardt brothers and Alfons Ancker, who wanted to place a 14 storey round glass office block at the top of the triangle between Bellevuestrasse and Potsdamerstrasse – exactly on the spot where today Potsdamer Platz joins the Sony centre.

Martin Wagner already envisaged an underground level for traffic and shops in his modern design for the re-modelling of Potsdamer Platz. The main idea of this area was to remove pedestrians from the busy traffic junction above, but the Columbus-Haus, designed by Erich Mendelsohn (1887–1953) and not completed until 1932, was the only part of such a grandiose vision to be realised. The 'new functionalism' ten storey steel structure on the corner of Ebertstrasse and Bellevuestrasse had been planned for the Parisian department store, Galeries Lafayette, but ended up mostly being used as an office block. A second building, also designed by Mendelsohn, was the Ufa film theatre on Lehniner Platz, which today houses the Schaubühne theatre.

More progressive buildings were being experimented with as an alternative to the tradtional tenement houses. A good example of this was the Hufeisensiedlung (horse-shoe estate) in Berlin-Britz, designed by the architects Bruno Taut (1880–1938) and Martin Wagner (1885–1957) and constructed between 1925 and 1927. An important feature was the large, green inner courtyards to give the apartments plenty of light and air.

Revue girls pose as the Quadriga in the Admiralpalast in Friedrichstrasse.

However, despite this and many other similar projects, there was still a housing shortage in Berlin because since the First World War an average of 80,000 people a year had moved to Berlin. Many large families continued to live in small dark apartments or had to make do with accommodation in barracks or summer houses.

Cinema, Radio, Cabaret

In the twenties a new consumerism began to develop which for the first time reached wider circles of the population, even it didn't quite become a real mass phenomenon. The car, the refrigerator and the vacuum cleaner were the first symbols of this culture and with the first household appliances came the gradual introduction of domestic electricity. In 1926 about 25 percent of households in Berlin had electricity but in 1932 it was already about 75 percent. Radio experienced a similar development and soon became a serious competitor for the Tageszeitung, the leading news medium. In 1923 the first radio programmes were broadcast from Vox-Haus on Potsdamer Platz. Two years later there were 269,000 registered receivers and this figure had risen to 854,000 in 1932. The first radio exhibition was held in 1924 and the Funkturm (radio tower), still today the symbol of the Berlin exhibition area, was officially opened in 1926.

Radios and other mass-produced goods were put on sale in newly designed temples of consumerism. The Karstadt department store on Hermannplatz, designed by Philipp Schäfer and built of iron, was the largest store in Europe and its spacious roof terrace attracted great acclaim.

It must be remembered, however, that many of these phenomena did not reach the wider public because far too many people still lived in very basic conditions. The stabilisation phase after 1923 was too short to reach all sections of the population. Towards the end of the decade the situation became even more critical and in 1929, the year of the world economic crisis, 25 percent of Berliners were surviving on public charity. The picture of the Golden Twenties is, therefore, in many ways a complete myth and the cinema played a significant role in perpetuating this myth.

The new medium of film was attractive and accessible for all classes of society. In 1919 alone the authorities received applications for the construction of 615 cinemas and Berlin soon developed into a film capital. Born as Maria Magdalena von Losch in Schöneberg, Marlene Dietrich (1901–1992) began her rise to international stardom in the Berlin of the twenties. Her greatest success was in 1930 in the film "Der Blaue Engel" (The Blue Angel) acting alongside Emil Jannings and directed by Josef von Sternberg, who smoothed the way to Hollywood for her. The producers, "Universum-Film-AG" (UFA), with studios just outside the city in Neubabelsberg and in Tempelhof, was one of the largest film companies of the time. The UFA belonged to the Hugenberg media empire. In 1916, with the help of credit and donations, Alfred Hugenberg (1865–1951) had bought the Scherl publishing house and with his press agencies such as the Telegraphen-Union or the ALA advertising agencies he had become one of the most influential right-wing opinion-makers in the Weimar Republic. In 1925 his press agencies supplied 40 percent of German newspapers with their content and with his power over the media Hugenberg was, in fact, partly responsible for the rise of a man who was to radically change the course of German history as no other ever had – Adolf Hitler. The Harzburger Front, initiated by Hugenberg and consisting of conservative and right-wing radical opponents of the young Weimar Rebublic, helped to make National Socialism become socially acceptable.

Back in Imperial days, Mosse, who published the renowned "Berliner Tageblatt" and Ullstein, with the "Vossische Zeitung", the "Berliner Morgenpost" and the "Berliner Illustrirte Zeitung" were also among the newspaper giants, together with the August Scherl publishing house. Their supremacy endured throughout the twenties and in 1926 the newspapers with the largest circulation were the "Berliner Morgenpost" with 600,000 and the Berliner Tageblatt with 300,000. At its peak the "Berliner Illustrirte Zeitung" was selling up to 1.6 million copies daily. The self-confidence of the press tsars was clearly reflected in the prestigious publishing houses like the one owned by Mosse on the corner of Jerusalemer Strasse and Schützenstrasse or the newly erected Ullstein printing house in Berliner Strasse (today Mariendorfer Damm) in Tempelhof.

Another social climber of the post-war period was the well-known left-wing press tsar, Willi Münzenberg, who soon became known as "red Hugenberg". With the "Welt

The Mosse-Haus, at the corner of Jerusalemer and Schützenstrasse.

am Abend" (Evening World), the "Welt am Morgen" (Morning World) and the "Arbeiter-Illustrierte Zeitung" (Workers' Illustrated Newspaper) which sold up to 400,000 copies a week, he became Hugenberg's first serious contender from the left-wing camp. Neither Hugenberg nor Münzenberg were well-disposed towards the Republic and therefore they can be seen to represent the polarisation and radicalisation within Weimar society which in the end drove it towards its doom.

Newspaper readers especially enjoyed the theatre reviews by distinguished writers like Kurt Tucholsky, Alfred Kerr and Maximilian Harden. They reflected the lively theatre scene in Berlin, which by now had over 50 theatres. Max Reinhardt was still improving the style of productions at the Deutsches Theatre and also worked at the Grosses Schauspielhaus and the Kammerspiele. In 1931 he took over the Komödie am Kurfürstendamm, the Berliner Theater and the Theater am Kurfürstendamm. Playwrights who had been active before the First World War were only just starting to celebrate their first big hits, for example Carl Sternheim "Die Hose"and "Bürger Schippel" and Georg Kaiser (1878–1945) "Die Bürger von Calais" and "Von morgens bis mitternachts", who had both laid the foundations of their reputation with works written in Imperial Germany.

One of Max Reinhardt's former actors, Erwin Piscator (1893–1966), wanted to create art for the masses through theatre. In 1921 he founded the Proletarian Theatre and performed only in front of workers. From 1924 until 1927 he was the Director of the Volksbühne and created quite a stir with his biting criticism of social conditions and the introduction of unconventional techniques such as the use of film scenes.

The literary view of a decade

When we think of culture in the Weimar Republic it is above all the names of writers that spring to mind – Bertolt Brecht, Arnold Zweig, Arnolt Bronnen, Gottfried Benn, Nelly Sachs or Erich Kästner. Many of them dealt with issues associated with the modern city in their works. In 1929 Alfred Döblin (1878–1957) described the scene in his panorama of the modern city "Berlin Alexanderplatz"(1929):

"On the Alexanderplatz they are tearing up the road-bed for the underground. People walk on planks. The tram-cars pass over the square up Alexanderstrasse through Münzstrasse to the Rosenthaler Tor. To the right and left are streets. They are full of men and women from cellar to garret. On the ground

Photo collage: „Symphony of a city", 1927.

floor are shops. Liquor shops, restaurants, fruit and vegetable stores, groceries and delicatessen, moving business, painting and decoration, manufacturing of ladies' wear, flour and mill materials, automobile garage, extinguisher company: The superiority of the small motor fire extinguisher lies in its simple constructions, easy service, small weight, small size – German fellow-citizens, never has a people been betrayed more ignominiously and more unjustly than the German people. Do you remember how Scheidemann promised us peace liberty, and bread from the window of the Reichstag on November 9th, 1918? And how that promise has been kept? – Drainage equipment, window-cleaning company, sleep is medicine, Steiner's Paradise Bed."

By 1933 50,000 copies of Döblin's novel had been bought in Germany alone and shortly after its publication "Berlin Alexanderplatz" was translated into many other languages. In 1931 it was made into a film in the UFA studios in Neubabelsberg and on location in Berlin, directed by Phil Jutzi with Heinrich George playing the main role.

Hans Fallada's novel "Kleiner Mann – was nun" (1932) (Little Man – what now?) was meant to be a memorial to a newly emerged social group – the white collar workers. Three years previously Siegfried

Kracauer had written: "Similar social conditions exist for large sections of white collar workers as for the actual proletariat. An industrial reserve army of employees has been formed." Hans Fallada's hero, Johannes Pinneberg, lived with the perpetual threat of unemployment and social descent and in fact this situation now applied to many women white collar workers, office employees and shop assistants. They earned between 10 and 15 percent less than men and worked a 48 hour week with no right to annual holiday. Irmgard Keun's novel "Das kunstseidene Mädchen" (The artificial silk girl) epitomises the Berlin working woman.

Democracy in defence

In 1924 the number of unemployed had gone down to 70,000 but by 1926 it had reached 230,000 again and until 1929 it fluctuated between 150,000 and 200,000. At the beginning of April 1932 there were 603,000 people registered as unemployed out of a population of 4,3 million (1929/30 census figures).

1929

The city council elections on 17th November 1929 had not resulted in any really sensational changes but they reflected the trend of the time. The Social Democrats remained the strongest party with 64 seats, but the Communists with 56 seats as well as the DNVP with 40 and the NSDAP with 13, represented a radicalisation of the city parliament.

Berlin was generally accepted as a stronghold of the "reds" and in 1926 the Nazis saw the appointment of Joseph Goebbels (1897–1945) as Gauleiter (Head of a Nazi administration district) as the beginning of their battle for Berlin. It was the spectacular street fights and brawls which first attracted attention to the Nazis and their SA. Goebbels first gave the signal for this battle with his appearance in the Pharussälen (Pharus Rooms) in Müllerstrasse in the borough of Wedding. It was here that the Communists had always held their meetings and now Goebbels' SA troops were disputing their right to do so. The Nazi writer Wilfrid Bade (1906–1945) later described this event as, "an evening that decided the way forward in Berlin. The march of the German freedom movement into the German capital had begun."

Whilst the public was very aware of these street fights in working-class boroughs between right-wing and left-wing elements, the majority of the proletariat remained on the left and in the 1930 elections the NSDAP had more success in the middle-class boroughs. The publication of "Der Angriff" (The Attack), a campaign leaflet produced by Goebbels himself, whose biting propaganda was a crusade against the Republic and its representatives, played a decisive role in the "conquest of the city".

The National Socialists also exploited the consequences of the world economic crisis. In the early thirties the economic situation in Berlin was hardly rosy. Just before Christmas 1931 the Borsig Works had to stop paying their workforce and the Berlin authorities had to sell off shares in the municipal electricity company BEWAG in order to make it pay. The final crisis in local government was the BVG strike in 1932 in which both Communists and National Socialists protested to the city authorities about the announced pay cuts. There were armed confrontations resulting in one death and several serious injuries,

Election workers with posters for the general election in July 1932.

but the direct consequences of the strike were minor; what was more significant was the symbolic strength of the two groups joining forces in their opposition to the Republic.

The crisis in the Republic was especially noticeable in Berlin, even if the Prussian State under its Social Democrat President, Otto Braun, remained an important pillar of democracy. Franz von Papen, the German Chancellor appointed by Hindenburg, used the street riots of 20th July 1932 as a reason to depose Braun's government. With this coup d'état from above, the so-called "Preussenschlag" (Prussian blow), Papen had effectively removed the last bastion of democracy.

The election that followed soon afterwards brought an absolute majority for the anti-democratic forces in parliament for the first time. The NSDAP gained 37.4 percent of the votes, the KPD 14.6 percent. However the end of the Weimar Republic did not come until Adolf Hitler was appointed German Chancellor on 30th January 1933. The Nazis celebrated this day, which they later inaccurately named the "Machtergreifung" (Seizure of Power), in typical fashion: a torchlight procession of SA troops marching through the Brandenburg Gate into Wilhelmstrasse.

From "Sieg Heil" into ruin

Berlin under the Nazis

The Nazis conquer the city

1933

This is the entry made by Joseph Goebbels, Gauleiter of Berlin, in his diary on 31st January 1933: "We have made it. We are sitting in Wilhelmstrasse. Hitler is German Chancellor. It is like a fairy-tale. Yesterday at noon, Kaiserhof: We are all waiting. At last he comes. Result: He German Chancellor, Frick German Home Office, Göring Prussian Home Office. The old man has given in. He was quite moved at the end. That's how it should be. Now we must win him over completely. We all have tears in our eyes. We shake Hitler's hand. He's deserved it. Great jubilation. The people are rioting below. Straight to work. The Reichstag is being dissolved. New elections in four weeks."

On that evening, the "old man", German President, Paul von Hindenburg (1847–1934) had appointed Hitler as German Chancellor. The most powerful man in the new cabinet was at that time Alfred Hugenberg, the press tsar. Goebbels remarked on this in his records as follows: "These are blemishes. They must be eradicated." In fact the two Nazis in the cabinet, Wilhelm Frick and Hermann Göring, as Home Secretary for Germany and Prussia respectively, held really key positions – they were responsible for the security forces across the country.

The fact that the Nazis used Berlin as one of their most important political theatres should not be confused with the fact that the city was at this stage by no means a Nazi stronghold. In the Reichstag elections in November 25.9 percent Berliners had voted for the NSDAP but 31percent had voted for the KPD. By contrast, in Germany as a whole the Nazis gained 33percent of the vote in this election and the Communists only 16.8 percent. But above all, these figures illustrate one thing – the majority of the votes had gone to the opponents of the Republic. Despite the propaganda put out by Goebbels, the party apparatus of the NSDAP in Berlin was comparatively quite weak. In 1931 the Greater Berlin "Gau" (Nazi district) had 16,000 Nazi members whereas at the same time over 40,000 were registered in Sachsen. But the Nazis in the German capital were well organised and the SA was considered particularly hard and "sturmerprobt" (experienced in assault).

The Nazis had access to the Prussian Police apparatus through Göring and after Göring had visited the Berlin Police Headquarters, the Police Chief currently in office

The torchlight procession organised by the National Socialists on the evening of 30th January 1933.

was replaced by a Nazi Party colleague. The intention was to use the police in action against "enemies of the state", as defined by the Nazis. Loyal police officers were dismissed in large numbers and replaced by "Auxiliary Police" from the ranks of the SA and SS.

Against this background the SA were now able to turn on their political opponents without any interference. All over Germany there were attacks against Social Democrats, Communists, "undesirable" intellectuals and Jewish citizens. Within a short space of time not only were numerous so-called "wild" concentration camps set up in Berlin but in the SA assault centres, their former assembly rooms, brutality and murder took place.

The Nazis themselves quickly set up the legal framework to deal with these riots. On 28th February 1933, after the Reichstag fire the previous day, there was a cabinet resolution called by the German President von Hindenburg to pass a "decree to protect the people and the state" which was directed against "traitors to the German people and treasonable machinations". The basic political rights of the Weimar constitution were effectively rescinded and a kind of state of emergency declared. The question of who was behind the arson attack on the Reichstag has to this day never been finally clarified, but this did not affect the way that the Nazis made political use of it. The Dutchman, Marinus van der Lubbe, was publicly presented as the perpetrator and on 23rd December 1933 he was sentenced to death by the High Court in Leipzig.

During the night of the Reichstag fire, thousands of opposition politicians were arrested and many were later taken off to the concentration camp at Oranienburg, to the north of Berlin. There were also other such prisons in the city centre which were mostly only in use until May 1933. The most notorious of these were the Columbiahaus at Tempelhof Airport which was run by the SS, the Headquarters of the SA leadership in Hedemannstrasse in Kreuzberg and the Headquarters of the SA field police in General-Pape-Strasse in Tempelhof. At least 23 people were murdered in the so-called Köpenicker blood week, an SA attack in June 1933. The SA had dragged them off to their assault centres as well as to the district court prisons. Most of them were members of the SPD or the KPD and among them was the former Social Democrat President of Mecklenburg, Johannes Stelling. A further 70 victims disappeared without trace and were probably also murdered.

Despite massive brutality the National Socialists did not gain an absolute majority in the Reichstag elections of 5th March 1933; in Germany they gained 43.9 percent and in Berlin only 34.6 percent. However, with their coalition partner DNVP, they achieved an overall majority of 51.9 percent nationwide.

Forcing everyone into line and the persecution of the Jews

The National Socialists took the last step on their way to absolute power in Germany with the staging of the Potsdam Day. In a solemn state ceremony in the Potsdam Garnisonkirche (Garrison Church) on 21st March 1933 the German Chancellor, Adolf Hitler, demonstrated his respect for the former Field Marshal and current German President Paul von Hindenburg. This show of solidarity between traditional Prussia and the National Socialist movement was supposed to reconcile conservative and middle-class circles with the new leadership. A postcard circulated at the time depicted Hitler alongside Friedrich II and Bismarck; a piece of propaganda intended to pave the way for the passing of the "Act removing the plight of the people and the State" (Ermächtigungsgesetz – Enabling Act). This Act, passed two days later, was the final business conducted by the Reichstag which now met in the Kroll opera house. The SPD members of the Reichstag opposed it and the KPD members had all been arrested. The Act allowed Hitler to pass laws without having to seek the agreement of parliament or the counter-signature of the German President; the State under the rule of law and the constitution of the Weimar Republic were thereby removed.

Measures were now introduced which could only be described as a way of forcing everyone into line ("Gleichschaltung"). They also affected the structure of local government administration. The Lord Mayor of Berlin, Heinrich Sahm, remained in office for the time being, probably because he was a member of the DNVP and was on good terms with Hindenburg. However, a State Commissioner with unlimited powers was put in place in order to single out all the undesirable civil servants within the city administration. Julius Lippert, the former Chairman of the NSDAP city councillors, fulfilled this function perfectly.

Behind the drive to "force the States into line with the nation" was a coup d'état from above against the Federal structures in Germany, concealed by virtue of the Enabling Act. Later the concept was broadened to include any measures used to bring organisations, institutions, unions and clubs into line with the new balance of power or, as was sadly often the case, any measures which the new rulers chose to adopt. This kind of "forcing into line" affected everyone, from small animal breeders to writers.

NSDAP campaigns were planned by the general staff and assisted by propaganda. For this purpose the Nazis had created a new Ministry of Propaganda run by the Gauleiter of Berlin Joseph Goebbels since 13th March 1933. This ministry had its powers transferred from various portfolios of other authorities and in this way it was able, over time, to gain enormous influence over the press, the radio, the cinema as well as all other creative arts.

The Minister's first big appearance was on the day of the "burning of the books" in Berlin, organised by the student body. Here, on 10th May 1933, the "12 theses against the un-German spirit" were proclaimed before the works of outlawed authors were thrown into the flames on the Opernplatz. Among them were books by Karl Marx, Sigmund Freud, Heinrich and Thomas Mann, Erich Kästner, Erich Maria Remarque, Carl von

The call for a "Jew Boycott" on 1st April 1933.

Ossietzky and Kurt Tucholsky, all of whose works were banned.

Among the first victims of the new regime in Berlin and all over the country were the Jews. The "Jew Boycott" on 1st April 1933 had made it clear that the initial despotic acts were not a question of individual attacks, but that the Nazis were aiming towards the systematic exclusion of Jews from German society. On this day the NSDAP had called for a boycott of all Jewish businesses, doctors and lawyers. SA troops were positioned in front of Jewish shops to add extra emphasis to the message, using force if necessary.

"I had an experience of this kind in Schlossstrasse in Steglitz", recalled Bernt von Kügelgen. " In the summer of 1934 I went there to buy something and saw a huge Star of David smeared across the whole shop window. Behind it I could see the shadowy

View across the spectator stands of the Olympic Stadium in August 1936.

figure of the owner, standing at the counter looking sadly out at the street. He had nothing to do. No customers came. (...) A few weeks later I had no trouble entering the shop. The Jewish owner had been removed and the shop expropriated. A stranger, an 'Aryan', stood in front of the decoratively arranged coloured pencils. From then on I made my purchases in the Kaufhaus des Westen on Wittenbergplatz."

At this time there were about 500,000 Jews living in Germany, a third of them in Berlin. However, they had a disproportional influence on the academic, economic and cultural life of the city and had made a significant contribution to the productive years of the Weimar Republic. Among them were Albert Einstein and Max Reinhardt as well as the distinguished publishers Samuel Fischer, Rudolf Mosse or the Editor-in-Chief of the "Berliner Tageblatt", Theodor Wolff. They were all banned from their profession, excluded from public life and had their businesses expropriated.

The Acts of Nuremberg finally degraded German Jews as second class citizens. These acts, passed on the day of the Nazi Party Convention in 1935, included a clause that made marriage between Jews and "those of German blood" a punishable offence. "Reichsbürgerschaft" (citizenship of the Third Reich) was now more important than state citizenship, which meant that being an Aryan held special political powers not granted to Jews, as merely citizens of the state. The persecution of the Jews was continually intensified right up to the so-called "Reichskristallnacht" (Crystal Night) on the night of 9th/10th November 1938 in which the Nazis organised a pogrom throughout Germany. During this night the majority of the remaining Jewish shops in Berlin were destroyed, the Berlin synagogues set on fire and 12,000 Jews from Berlin were deported to concentration camps. After these events in November the strength of the emigration movement increased. In 1933 there were about 160,000 Jews in the city, 3.8 percent of the population. In 1937, after the first exodus of emigrants, it was still 140,000 and then in July 1939 there remained about 75,000.

It was from Berlin that the National Socialists planned and organised their greatest crime; the systematic mass murder of the Jews in Europe. On 20th January 1942 the "Wannsee-Konferenz" took place in one of the villas used by the Reichssicherheitshauptamt (RSHA – State Security Service) situated by the Grosser Wannsee lake. Various officials in this organisation and members of the SS, including Reinhard Heydrich and Adolf Eichmann, met on this day to clarify questions that had already arisen in connection with the mass murders begun in Eastern Europe. The crime was euphemistically called the "Endlösung der Judenfrage" (The final solution to the Jewish question). Today, there is a memorial and educational exhibition in the villa at 56–58 Am Grossen Wannsee, which aims to keep the memory of the Holocaust alive.

From the "Peoples' Festival" to "Germania"

Terror and repression alone could not have kept the regime in power, they also needed to create opportunities for more positive identification with what they represented. As capital of the new Germany which had emerged from the world economic crisis and the battles of the Weimar Republic, Berlin provided the best backdrop for this purpose.

The XI Olympics Games, held in Berlin in 1936, had already been planned before the Nazis came to power and despite numerous demands to boycott them they still took place and were used by the regime as a massive propaganda exercise. Anti-semitic slogans were removed from the city for the duration of the Games and the sale of the rabble-rousing newspaper, "Der Stürmer", was prohibited with the aim of leading the international community to believe for the last time in a picture of a peaceful Germany. The Reichsportfeld designed by Werner and Walter March, which included the Olympic Stadium, an open-air theatre (today "Waldbühne"), and a parade ground ("Maifeld") was one of the first constructions of the Third Reich. Even if the original planning went back to the time well before the Nazis had come to power they still managed to sell the new Olympic complex as their own achieve-

Model of the Grosse Halle designed by Albert Speer

The German Air Ministry in Wilhelmstrasse.

ment. This was mainly possible through clever use of the modern media of radio, film and, in an experimental phase, even television. It was above all the media depiction of the "great deeds" that attracted positive attention to the regime's image all over the world. There were 368 radio broadcasts of the Olympics in Europe and almost 800 further afield. Leni Riefenstahl (1902–2003) erected a lasting cinematic monument to the event with her two part film of the Olympics, "Fest der Völker" (The Peoples' Festival) which was premiered on 20th April 1938 in the UFA-Palast am Zoo cinema.

During the Olympics the shady side of the regime was only hidden, not really put in a good light. For example the Games were used as a opportunity to intern all the Sinti and Roma (gypsies) from Berlin in a camp in Marzahn from which they were later deported to the extermination camp in Auschwitz.

Berlin's 700th Anniversary celebrations in 1937 offered the next great opportunity for self-aggrandisement when Goebbels, Gauleiter and "first man by the Spree", took centre stage. A rather curious heirloom from this year is the living Berlin heraldic animal in his bear cage behind the Märkisches Museum. This all goes back to a campaign started by an "open letter to city father Lippert" during the 700th Anniversary celebrations and whose cause the tabloid newspaper BZ subsequently took up. In the letter the writer claimed that something was missing from the Berliners' happiness: "... we don't have a living Berlin bear who belongs to us Berliners alone and to whom we can take our friends from other towns and countries. Then we can stand in front of the cage and softly say: Come here, Petz and say good day to the gentleman, he has come all the way from London! So we know that this is not a vain request – dear father Lippert, give the Berliners their bear."

One of the large building projects inspired by the new leadership was the terminal building at Tempelhof Airport which still stands today. The architect, Ernst Sagebiel (1892–1970) was awarded the contract for this project in 1935. Although the airport was initially a municipal building the extension was so important to the Nazis as an international advertisement that they financed it with money taken from the armaments budget of the recently founded Air Ministry.

However, the planned projects were much more ambitious than those already realised. In the foreseeable future Berlin was to be the centre of power of a "great German world empire" and would then be called "Germania". An authority was created for this sole purpose, the "Generalbauinspektor für die Reichshaupstadt Berlin" (GBI –, General Building Inspectorate for Berlin, capital of the Reich) with Albert Speer (1905–1981) as its leader. In drawing up its plans the authority paid no heed to existing city structures. The main consideration was to be the road axes that ran through Berlin from east to west and from north to south. Speer had planned an enormous circular open space at the crossing of Potsdamer Strasse and the North-South axis. The demolition of whole apartment blocks in the Alsen district on Linkstrasse and Potsdamer Strasse were part of the preparatory measures which actually took place.

Traces of the work on the East-West-Axis can still be seen today; the candelabra street lamps on Bismarck Strasse and Strasse des 17. Juni as well as the Siegessäule (Victory Column) which now stands in the middle of the Grosser Stern. Until 1939 it stood on Königsplatz directly in front of the Reichstag, but was moved to be more visible on the axis and raised by one column segment to be in line with the planned dimensions of the new city. A rather curious inheritance from this time is the so-called "Grossbelastungskörper" which may still be admired today in General-Pape-Strasse in Tempelhof. A round lump of concrete weighing several thousand tons was placed here to test the load-bearing capacity of the Brandenburg sand for a huge triumphal arch and it has survived both the bombing and attempts to demolish it.

At the heart of Germania was to have been the Grosse Halle des Volkes (Great Hall of the People) which would hold almost 180,000 people and was to stand near the Reichstag on the Spree. Its planned height was 300 metres, not far short of today's television tower at 365 metres!

Further traces of the Nazis' desire for prestige in their city architecture have disappeared in the aftermath of war, for example the Neue Reichskanzlei (New Reichschancellory) in Vossstrasse which was designed and built by Albert Speer and which Hitler used as his official headquarters from 1939 onwards. In the post-war period it was gradually demolished and finally some of its building materials have been recycled in today's Berlin; the marble and limestone was used in the construction of the Soviet War Memorial in Treptower Park as well as in the re-modelling of the Thälmannplatz underground station (formerly Kaiserhof), now Mohrenstrasse.

Around Wilhelmstrasse large sections of the Propaganda Ministry can still be seen today. Today, between Mauerstrasse and Wilhelmstrasse, it houses the Bundesministerium für Arbeit und Soziales (Federal Ministry for Work and Social Security). The Air Ministry on the corner of Leipzigerstrasse and Wilhelmstrasse designed by Ernst Sagebiel, today the headquarters of the Federal Finance Minister, just comes into a view a little further to the south. Directly next to it is the so-called Prinz-Albrecht-Gelände, bordered by Niederkirchnerstrasse, Wilhelmstrasse and Anhalterstrasse. On this land stood buildings used by the authorities which were largely responsible for carrying

1939

out Nazi crimes such as the Geheime Staatspolizei (Gestapo – Secret State Police) or the SS Reichsführer (Himmler). This plot of rubble and wasteland has served for many years as the documentation centre "Topographie des Terrors" whose aim is to educate and enlighten.

Bombing and resistance

When the Second World War began on 1st September 1939 with the invasion of Poland there was not the same enthusiasm for war on the streets of Berlin as there had been in 1914.

From the very beginning of the war the population had to keep strictly to the black-out and this meant that both private and public life became limited. Ration cards were introduced to keep a firm control on food supplies and the Berliners realised how serious the situation was in Spring 1940 when they were encouraged to use open spaces, gardens and parks for growing vegetables. The most well-known of these was certainly the Gendarmenmarkt potato "allotment".

The German Luftwaffe had already started attacking targets in England at the start of August 1940 and the bombing raid on Berlin during the night of 25/26th August 1940 was an act of retaliation. However only a few aircraft hit their target and about 22 tons of bombs fell in the north of the city. In reaction to this attack on 9th September, Hitler ordered flak towers to be built all over Berlin which were supposed to prevent or discourage enemy aircraft from flying over the city centre. The huge constructions at the Zoo and at Humboldthain and Friedrichshain were erected between October 1940 and April 1942. It is possible to imagine just how gigantic these structures were; at Gesundbrunnen underground station in the Humboldthain Volkspark there is still part of a flak tower which rises up into the Berlin sky and serves as a viewing platform.

Despite the relatively small range of the British bombers, by the end of September 1940 over 500 Berliners had already been killed and more than 1,600 buildings had been totally destroyed. 1941 and 1942 were quieter as far as the bombing went – there were certainly fewer air-raid alarms. But there was still some serious damage, including at Potsdam Station and Potsdamer Platz, although there was no further blanket bombing as the British Royal Air Force were concentrating their efforts on the Ruhrgebiet and Northern Germany for the time being.

In March 1943 700 Berliners died as a result of more intensive attacks on the city, but things took a turn for the worse for Berlin in the summer of 1943. The figures from the 16 large bombing raids carried out by the British and Americans in the "Battle of Berlin" make terrible reading; the RAF lost 4,000 men, there were 6,166 deaths on the ground and 18,431 seriously injured. 1.5 million Berliners were left homeless and 9.5 square kilometres of the city were destroyed. There were repeated bombing raids on government buildings and the headquarters of the administration in the city centre and the industrial centres, such as the Daimler-Benz factory in Marienfelde and parts of the Siemens Works in Siemensstadt, also became targets. Other areas affected were the densely populated residential quarters around

Alexanderplatz, the Hansaviertel and Charlottenburg, to name only a few.

The final death toll from the bombing of Berlin was 50,000. Greater Berlin lost 39 percent of its housing and 28.5 square kilometres of the city were reduced to rubble. The worst affected borough was Berlin-Mitte where 70 percent of the housing was destroyed.

The persecution of the Berlin Jews also intensified during the war. After the Wehrmacht (German Army) had invaded the Soviet Union and the USA been forced entered the war it seemed as if the Nazis knew no limits. Many Jews had already been forced to leave their homes in April 1939 and had been herded into ghettos – so-called Jewish houses. On 18th October 1941 the deportation of Berlin Jews to Auschwitz and other concentration and extermination camps began. The transport trains left from the goods stations of Putlitzstrasse and Grunewald. Of the 73,000 Jews who had remained in Berlin there were only 6,000 left after the war, most of whom had been protected by a non-Jewish partner and about 1,400 had managed to survive in illegal hiding-places.

Berlin is often described as the centre of resistance during the Nazi period. Traditionally a left-wing stronghold, the city actually harboured a considerable number of resistance groups and offered a certain anonymity for illegal activities. The most well-known of these groups was the "Rote Kapelle" (Red Chapel) led by Arvid Harnack (1901–1942) and Harro Schulze-Boysen (1909–1942). In the spring of 1941 Harnack and Schulze-Boysen warned the Soviet positions of the German preparations for attack and in the autumn of the following year 120 members of the Rote Kapelle were arrested

Clearing up after an air raid in Alt-Moabit

and 49 of them condemned to death, including Harnack and Schulze-Boysen. They were executed in Plötzensee prison.

Alongside this resistance group, the "Bekennende Kirche" (Confessional Church) led by the Dahlem priest, Martin Niemöller and the Saefkow-Jacob Group, started by the former KPD officers Anton Saefkow and Franz Jacob, also had Berlin as their centre.

Even the assassination attempt of 20th July 1944 is connected with the German capital. This is, of course, mainly because the government and control centres against which the coup d'état was planned, were in Berlin. In fact, the bomb smuggled in by

Claus Graf Schenk von Stauffenberg was detonated in the Führer's Headquarters in East Prussia, whereas on that day the logistics centre of the conspirators, to whom the Social Democrat Julius Leber (1891–1945) and the the former Mayor of Leipzig, Carl Friedrich Goerdeler (1884–1945) belonged, was in the Bendlerblock, which contained the office of the Commander of the Reserve Army. Today, with its view on to the Landwehrkanal, it is home to the Federal Ministry of Defence which likes to use the example of resistance fighters such as von Stauffenberg, some of the few well-known representatives of the other Germany in Nazi times, to reinforce a sense of tradition within the Bundeswehr (Federal Army). As a reaction to the failed coup d'état of 20th July there was a wholesale rounding-up of all the supporters and sympathisers in which 700 people were arrested and 180 subsequently executed.

The attempt to protect Germany from total defeat had failed. The German Reich was now retreating on every front.

The End

1945

At this stage the Allies were already discussing the new political order of post-war Europe. At the Conference of Yalta (4th to 11th February 1945) the leaders of Great Britain, the USSR and the USA signed the "London Treaty". This dictated that the area of Greater Berlin would be mapped out according to the administrative reforms of 1920 and then divided up into three sectors for each of the victorious powers.

On 1st February 1945 the Nazis declared Berlin a "defence area". Berlin was to be turned into a fortress by setting up defensive positions on the rivers Oder and Neiße, as well as three defensive belts in and around the city itself. The "Wachregiment Grossdeutschland" (Duty Regiment of Greater Germany), the 3rd and 4th Tank Regiments as well as the 9th Army, were all standing by. They were to be supported by members of the German Territorial Army, old men, youths and children. On 16th April the final Battle for Berlin began with the battle on the Seelower Hills, 50 kilometres east of Berlin. Just a few days later the Red Army reached the northern edge of the city. The demand to surrender was initially refused, so the Soviet troops slowly fought their way through the streets towards the city centre.

The defeat of the Third Reich could no longer be reversed. Even the last newspaper published on the front "Der Panzerbär" which was printed in Berlin between 22nd and 29th April to urge the population to hold out against the enemy, could not change anything and on 30th April Hitler committed suicide in his bunker under the Reichschancellory. Shortly afterwards, the Gauleiter of Berlin, who two years previously had declared "total war" from the Sportpalast, also killed both himself and his family. The Military Governor of Berlin, General of the Artillery Helmuth Weidling finally surrendered on 2nd May 1945.

During the night of 8/9th May the surrender document was signed on behalf of the Commander-in-Chief of the Wehrmacht in the Soviet Headquarters in Berlin-Karlshorst; other partial surrenders and the signing of similar documents had already taken place in the US Headquarters in Reims. With these symbolic acts the Third Reich was finished.

Red Army soldiers hoist their flag on the Reichstag building. Photo by Jewgeni Chaldej, May 1945.

The Cold War and the Berlin Wall

The divided city

Life in ruins

Until the beginning of July 1945 the Soviet Union was the only occupying power in Berlin. Then the British, Americans and later the French, as the fourth power, arrived. Even if the political differences within the Anti-Hitler coalition had already become apparent for a long time, the victorious powers went ahead with their plans for a joint administration in Berlin. There was a joint governing authority, the "Komman-dantura", where the Commanders of the four occupying powers met. The corresponding treaty of 26th July 1945 between the govern-ments of the occupying powers stated that: "Germany, within its borders as they existed on 31st December 1937, is divided into four zones of occupation each if which is assigned to one of the four powers and into a special Berlin area, which is occupied by the four powers." The questions which affect-ed Germany as a whole were to be clarified by a newly installed Allied Control Council, which also had its headquarters in Berlin, in the former building of the Berlin Supreme Court in Kleistpark in the borough of Schöneberg. So far there had been no talk of division or new confrontation, at least not officially.

In 1945 most of the city centre painted a tragic picture. On Potsdamer Platz only a few buildings such as the Columbus-Haus had partly survived the war, but nevertheless some sort of city life was re-established incre-dibly quickly. At the intersection between the American, British and Soviet sectors a typical post-war black market developed, selling stockings, cigarettes, chocolate and other highly prized goods.

Large sections of the city's infrastructure had been destroyed. Local traffic had come to a standstill, there was neither gas nor electri-city and even the water supply did not func-tion properly. In June 1945 out of a previous total of 153,000 private vehicles there were only 115 still registered, 122 of the 166 bridges had been destroyed and only 9,000 of the 33,000 hospital beds could still be used. A symbolic figure of these times of survival were the "Trümmerfrauen" (the women who cleared away the rubble after the bombing), whose husbands had either been killed or were in prisoner of war camps. They tried to make everyday life possible among the ruins, cleared away the rubble, made the streets passable and picked out bricks from the mountains of rubble to re-build the city. They even managed provide for their families by going on foraging trips

Red Army soldier directing the traffic, Reichstag building in the background.

("Hamsterfahrten") into the surrounding countryside to exchange valuables for anything edible or they bargained at the various black markets. The food which was officially available was strictly rationed and insufficient to feed everyone adequately. The supply problems were further heightened by the addition of thousands of refugees flooding into Berlin.

The Beginning of the East West Confrontation

Until July the Soviet Armed Forces, under the Military Governor, General Nikolai Erastowitsch Bersarin (1904–1945), were solely responsible for the fate of the city and they had tried to set the course to suit their ends. For example, Bersarin had appointed a so-called anti-fascist municipal authority of whom the majority were in the communist camp and in most boroughs and in the police department all the key positions were similarly filled. The Soviets were supported by the Ulbricht Group which consisted of returned emigrants who had gathered around the KPD official, Walter Ulbricht (1898–1973). Wolfgang Leonard, one of Ulbricht's disciples at that time, recalls: "The Borough Councils must be politically correct in their composition. We don't need communist mayors, except possibly in Wedding or in Friedrichshain. The mayors of the working class boroughs should normally be Social

Democrats. In the middle class districts – Zehlendorf, Wilmersdorf, Charlottenburg and so on – we must put a middle class man in at the top, someone who belonged to the Demokratische Partei or the Deutsche Volkspartei".

In July and August the Western Allies moved into their Sectors. The Americans occupied Kreuzberg, Neukölln, Tempelhof, Schöneberg, Steglitz and Zehlendorf, the British Tiergarten, Wilmersdorf, Charlottenburg and Spandau and the French Wedding and Reinickendorf. Within the Allied Kommandantura the Soviets had managed to push through their demand that each of the Sectors should be supplied from their respective occupation zones and this *de facto* cut off the Western Sectors from their traditional surrounding countryside of Brandenburg.

At the Potsdam Conference from 17th July to 2nd August 1945, the leaders of the three big powers, the USA, USSR and Great Britain, met in the Schloss Cecilienhof to discuss Germany's political and economic future. Those present were Harry S. Truman, Jossif W. Stalin and Winston Churchill (who was replaced by Clement Attlee after his election defeat). They reached an agreement on how much each occupation zone should pay in the way of reparations and achieved an understanding about the basic principles of the democratisation and demilitarisation of Germany, which was now understood to exclude the former German territories east of the rivers Oder and Neisse.

In the first and last free city council elections in Berlin, in which both the SPD and the SED (which was the name given to forced merger of the SPD and KPD in the East Sector) were allowed to take part, there was a 90 percent turnout. The SPD gained 48.7% of the votes and the SED landed up in third place behind the CDU with 19.8%. In June 1947 the Soviet Union exercised their veto when Ernst Reuter (SPD) was elected Mayor of Berlin and Louise Schroeder (1887–1957) and Ferdinand Friedensburg (1886–1972) took his place for the time being.

On 20th June 1948, after joint currency negotiations between the four powers had failed, the Western Allies introduced a new currency in their own zones of occupation which shortly afterwards was also valid in the Western Sectors of Berlin. The representatives of the Soviet Union had already walked out of the Allied Control Council. A future for a unified Germany was looking less and less likely; separate paths were becoming apparent.

Blockade and Airlift

"Today is the day when the people of Berlin raise their voices. (....) You peoples of the world! You people in America, in England, France and Italy! Look at this city and realise that you mustn't abandon this people, can't abandon them!" With this emotional speech on 9th September 1948, the Mayor of Berlin, Ernst Reuter, appealed for international solidarity for the blockaded West Berlin. On 24th June of the same year, the day of the currency reform in the Western Sectors of the city, the Soviet military administration had cut off supplies by land and water to the western half of Berlin. The American Military Governor, Lucius D. Clay (1897–1978) reacted by setting up an airlift. Just two days later the first transport aircraft landed. The British

Ernst Reuter making his famous speech on 9th September 1948.

RAF took part in the flights as well and the French occupying power increased the transport capacities by building a new take-off and landing strip in Tegel. Clay calculated a daily requirement of 5,000 tons of essential goods. By the end of the blockade in October 1949, 2.3 million tons of goods had been flown to West Berlin on a total of 277,000 flights. The main cargo was coal (67 percent of the total goods transported) and food (24 percent) as well as medicines and raw materials. The Soviet Union allowed supplies to be brought in the usual way from May 1949 onwards, but the Western Allies con-tinued the flights until October. The so-called "Rosinenbomber", which flew into Tempelhof airport, were a symbol of the new atmosphere of friendship between the defeated and the victors.

70 members of the Allied forces and eight German helpers lost their lives in the Berlin Airlift and the "Luftbrücke" memorial at Tempelhof Airport commemorates both these victims and all those who took part in the Berlin Airlift.

The blockade put the final seal on any plans to retain a joint administration in Greater Berlin. On 16th June 1948 the Soviet side had left the Kommandantura as well and on 6th September demonstrators occupied the Town Hall. Those associated with the SED probably wanted to block the approaching new elections which looked as if they would turn out unfavourably for their party. The non-communist town councillors moved into the western part of the city and this resulted in the formation of two city parliaments and municipal authorities. In the Soviet Sector, Friedrich Ebert, the son of the former German President, was voted in as Mayor by an extraordinary meeting of the City Councillors. In West Berlin Ernst Reuter, who had already been elected in 1947, was once again the choice of the newly elected City Parliament and was finally able to take up his office as Mayor.

When the Basic Law came into force in the Federal Republic of Germany on 24th May 1949 and the German Democratic Republic was founded on 7th October of the same year, Germany was finally on the way to becoming two States and the former Greater Berlin was two cities. In their constitutions both the Federal Republic as well as the GDR claimed Berlin as their own. The federal side saw Greater Berlin as a Federal State like the others. For the GDR Berlin was the "Capital of the Democratic Republic". For decades the difference was noticeable in the official use of language; whilst in the West, people referred to Berlin (West) or West-Berlin with a hyphen, the East spoke of its capital proudly as "Berlin, Capital of the GDR" and might at best refer to the "political unit of Westberlin" (without hyphen), which often appeared on East Berlin maps as a white, empty space.

In the west the constitution approved by the Allies came into force in Berlin, although the requirements of Article 1 which stated that, "Berlin is a state of the Federal Republic of Germany and the Basic Law and laws of the Federal Republic of Germany are also binding for Berlin", was at first rejected by the Allies. Berlin had *de facto* a special status, so there were areas where, if there was a conflict between the Allied and Berlin law, the latter could be revoked. This was particularly relevant in the interests of security, in questions of demilitarisation or with regard to the powers of the police. The most amazing aspect of this special status was the fact that in October 1951 the Western Allies ruled that for various crimes, for example armed resistance against occupation force, they could impose the death penalty, which was not contained in the Basic Law of the Federal Republic. In actual fact, it was part of Allied special rights that were never put into practice.

A direct result of the Berlin Blockade was the setting up of the Berlin stocks. Financed partly by a Senate reserve and partly by a Federal reserve, these stocks meant that the city could be supplied with essential goods for an extended period of time. There were 250 stores, the largest of which was on the Westhafen site, and the stocks included fuel, grain, clothing, foodstuffs and even bicycles and tooth gold.

In the Cold War

In both halves of the city reconstruction and clearing of the war rubble was being gradually completed. The situation for the island of West Berlin had become especially precarious and with 306,000 unemployed, the crisis had reached its high point there in 1950. The Berlin construction programme, which was financed from European and Federal funds and which aimed to remove all the war damage and build new housing, acted as a counterbalance. Without its strong ties with the Federal Republic the city would not have been able to survive. Their united efforts soon bore fruit and the upward trend of the economic miracle in the Federal Republic also began to have delayed effects in Berlin. In 1957 100,000 homes built since the end of the war were ready for occupation and in the same year 1,200 new dwellings in the Hansaviertel, which had been built for the framework of the International Building Exhibition, were handed over to the public. The most prominent building created during this period was the Congress Hall in the Tiergarten, today the House of World Cultures. It was financed with money from the American Benjamin Franklin Foundations as well as funds from the Federal Republic and the Berlin Senate.

In the east of the city there was also war damage to be removed and repaired; 20 million cubic metres of rubble had to be cleared away. However, in the process of these works, buildings which could easily have been repaired were removed for political reasons, including the Stadtschloss of the Hohenzollern where demolition began in 1950. Only the Portal IV, from which Karl Liebknecht proclaimed the Free Socialist Republic on 9th November 1918, was to be preserved and between 1962–1964 it was integrated into the newly erected Council of State building, just south of the site of the palace, as the official entrance.

The most well-known reconstruction works of the early years of East Berlin were on Frankfurter Allee, which was then still called Stalinallee. The chief architect was Hermann Henselmann who supervised the construction of distinctive modern blocks of appartments and shops. Even today, a stroll between Frankfurter Tor and Strausberger Platz gives the impressive feel of a ceremonial avenue typical of Eastern European cities.

View from the tower of the Rotes Rathaus, September 1946.

Taking a walk along Stalinallee, April 1953.

17th June 1953

According to popular opinion, the uprising of 17th June 1953 started on the Stalinallee, but in fact it was building workers at the Friedrichshain Hospital who first took industrial action. Their demands to lower the "quotas", i.e. the work output that had been fixed by government decree, were also echoed by colleagues working on Stalinallee and on the State Opera House in Unter den Linden. Within a few hours it developed into a protest movement that spread from Berlin into the whole of the GDR and made the Western Allies extremely worried. Demands such as "Lower the quotas!", rapidly turned into slogans like "Colleagues get in line, we want to be free people!" or "Get the government out!"

Pictures of this uprising have ensured that for a long time the 17th June was seen as a phenomenon that only occurred in the former capital, because nearly all the photos and films were taken in Leipziger Strasse in East Berlin. Camera teams and journalists in the western part of the city had mostly taken up positions at Potsdamer Platz where they could get a good view along the length of Leipziger Strasse by using a telephoto lens and binoculars. For example, they were able to see from a safe distance the street in front of the Haus der Ministerien (House of Ministries) the former Air Ministry, where on 16th and 17th June thousands gathered to present their demands to the GDR Government.

By 1953 Berlin had already developed into a place where the East and the West competed with each other side by side; it functioned as a shop window for both camps. A Berlin institution which owed its foundation in 1946 to this situation was RIAS (Rundfunk im amerikanischen Sektor – Radio in the American Sector). This radio station, initially financed by the American Federal German budget and since the end of the sixties by the Federal Ministry for Inner German Relations, was mainly intended to reach listeners in East Berlin and in the GDR. However, it wasn't just political programmes that interested the listeners; the theatre critic, Friedrich Luft, had a faithful following with his weekly broadcast, "Voice of the Critic" and so did compère, Hans Rosenthal, with his Sunday music quiz.

1953

In the summer of 1953 other messages were sent across the airwaves. The official report about the events in Berlin came to the conclusion that the protest movement on 17th June quickly spread to the rest of the GDR. On 16th June at 16.30 the radio station in Kufsteiner Strasse, Schöneberg (which today still bears the name RIAS) broadcast the following announcement: "In the Soviet Sector of Berlin there have been mass demonstrations by the workers who are protesting in front of the Zone Government building against the rise in working quotas, the conditions in the Soviet occupied sector and the politics of the government itself. The square in front of the government building is packed with people shouting: "We demand higher wages and lower prices. We demand the removal of quotas. Out with the government! We want free elections!"

The uprising was ended when the Soviet occupying forces declared a situation of martial law during the afternoon of 17th June. By banning meetings, imposing a curfew and putting a massive military presence on the streets they gradually restored peace and order. The result was further repression in the GDR; 13,000 people were arrested after the unrest, at least temporarily. Twelve demonstrators were killed in the clashes in East Berlin and over 400 were seriously injured. Among the Volkspolizei (GDR Police) there were over 200 injured, but there are no figures for injured Soviet soldiers.

Demonstrators in Leipzigerstrasse on the afternoon of 17th June 1953.

At the beginning of the fifties Berlin was still an open city. 60,000 West Berliners worked in East Berlin and almost the same number of East Berliners commuted to the west each day to earn their wages. When the border with the Federal Republic was closed in May 1952 it was still possible to pass freely across the sector borders in Berlin. In the first half of 1953 216,000 people fled from the GDR and a further 105,000 followed in the second half, despite the temporary closing of the inner-city border in Berlin. For the next few years the annual number of refugees was around 150,000.

Khrushchev-Ultimatum and the building of the Wall

In 1956 the Soviet Premier, Nikita Khrushchev, made it quite clear that Berlin was the place where the East-West confrontation would be played out: "Not only will an ideological war be fought there, but also an economic war between socialism and capitalism. It is there that the comparison will be made as to which regime has created the better material conditions – West Germany or East Germany."

Locals watching the building of the Wall in Bernauer Strasse.

In November 1958 people all over the world held their breath. In the so-called Khrushchev-Ultimatum, the Soviet Government demanded the demilitarisation of Berlin, which meant the withdrawal of the Western Allies as well as its transformation into a free city. The whole of Berlin was to become part of the GDR. If the Allies refused, the Kremlin maintained that the GDR Government would be given full sovereignty over their state territory. The Western Allies were worried that in this case the GDR Government would impose a complete blockade around the island of West Berlin, however they rejected the ultimatum – and there were no immediate consequences.

The next dramatic change in Berlin's situation was alluded to at a press conference in the Haus of Ministries in Leipzigerstrasse in June 1961. When a journalist from the "Frankfurter Rundschau" asked Walter Ulbricht what he meant by a "Free City of Berlin", he gave a highly significant answer: "I understand your question to mean that there are people in West Germany who would like us to mobilise the construction workers of the capital to build a wall. (...) No-one has the intention of building a wall!"

However, on 13th August 1961 the unthinkable happened: a city began to be sealed off.

GDR Border Guards and members of fighting units appeared everywhere. Local traffic was stopped and barriers were set up on the streets and squares along the sector borders. Only a few checkpoints remained

From 1963 onwards the Wall was strengthened with concrete in many places.

open, until 23rd August for West Berliners these were at Friedrichstrasse (S-Bahn station), Bornholmer Strasse, Chaussee-strasse, Invalidenstrasse, Heinrich-Heine Strasse, Oberbaumbrücke and Sonnenallee. Over the years, the provisional barriers and barbed wire fences were replaced with more and more perfect border installations.

From this time on, East Berliners were not allowed into the western sectors, either to work or on private visits. It also became impossible for West Berliners to visit East Berlin. Until the so-called visitors' treaty came into force in 1972, only short-term visits to East Berlin could be arranged under the permit regulations set up in 1963, 1964, 1965 and 1966. In the period after that, a permit office controlled urgent family visits for occasions such as marriages, births, serious illnesses or deaths.

As soon as construction on the Wall began, there were dramatic escape scenes at the inner-city border. By mid-September 600 people had managed to escape into West Berlin. They jumped over the fences, swam across the Spree or drove through the barriers in vehicles and the photograph of the GDR Border Guard, Conrad Schumann jumping over the barbed wire at Bernauer Strasse on 15th August became famous all over the world. Bernauer Strasse found itself in a particularly spectacular situation as the Wall ran down the middle of the street. After 13th August many East Berliners used the houses on the eastern side for escape purposes and it was here that the Wall claimed its first casu-

Potsdamer Platz, 1961.

alties. On 22nd August 59 year old Ida Siekmann suffered fatal injuries when she tried to jump into the western part of the city and three days earlier a 57 year old man tried to abseil across and died four weeks later from his injuries.

It took a long time for life to gradually return to normal on both sides of the Wall. At first the West Berliners were disappointed that the Western Allies had done nothing about the sealing-off of their city, but there was widespread fear of a confrontation that could have brought the world closer to another war. When their right of access to the eastern sector was threatened, the Western Allies only let things get as far as a trial of strength. The short-lived refusal of GDR Border guards to allow the Western Allies free passage through Checkpoint Charlie in Friedrichstrasse led to a confrontation between the USA and the USSR. On 26th October 1961 the Americans positioned tanks at Checkpoint Charlie, on the next day the Soviets followed suit and for two days they sat facing each other. However, it did not come to an armed conflict; both President Kennedy and Khrushchev made efforts to de-escalate the situation.

With their determined attitude the Western Allies had made it clear that they were not going to alter the Four Power status of Berlin and that they intended to retain their right to free movement between the sectors.

US President John F. Kennedy on a visit to the Brandenburg Gate in June 1963.

For the Berliners, however, it was a further two years before they were to receive their famous message of solidarity, when US President Kennedy came to their divided city in June 1963. He was welcomed by Willy Brandt (SPD), who was Mayor of Berlin from 1957 to 1966. On 26th June, in front of 300,000 people at Schöneberg Town Hall, Kennedy made his historic speech: "The wall is the most obvious and vivid demonstration of the failures of the Communist system (...) for it is, as your Mayor has said, an offense not only against history but an offense against humanity (...) All free men, wherever they may live, are citizens of Berlin, and, therefore, as a free man, I take pride in the words: Ich bin ein Berliner."

Living with the Berlin Wall

It wasn't just Kennedy who was taken to see the Wall (or "Anti-fascist Protection Wall" as it was referred to by the GDR), it became part of the official visitor programme in both the East and the West. Walter Ulbricht had shown it to Khrushchev in January 1963. A visit to the Wall also became a regular feature of ordinary visits to West Berlin and countless western tourists came to see this depressing sight of the former capital. When they climbed on to one of the viewing platforms at the sector border, for example somewhere like Potsdamer Platz that used to be such a hub of activity, they looked across an inner-city waste-land of vast proportions. Even on the West Berlin side there were hardly any buildings left and some quite presentable ruins, which could easily have been restored, including the remains of the Haus Vaterland at Potsdamer Station, had disappeared by the beginning of the seventies. One of the victims of this frenzy of demolition was the Vox-Haus at 4, Potsdamer Strasse, where the first German radio programme was transmitted in 1923. The sole buildings remaining in what was once such a lively area, were the Weinhaus Huth and the torso of the Grand Hotel Esplanade in Bellevuestrasse. The only sign of life was the Wall tourism at Potsdamer Platz and the souvenir shops there dated back to the stalls and bureaux de change from the time of the border traffic before the Wall was built.

The division of Berlin became more and more of a tourist attraction in the West and the Berliners themselves learned to live in a divided city. For one half an island existence became a reality, and the other half slowly came to terms with the white expanses on their maps.

However the Wall remained a deathly construction; it claimed the lives of 239 people trying to escape into West Berlin. One of the most well-known victims was Peter Fechter, who died at the Wall in August 1962. Together with a colleague, he had tried to get across to the West in Zimmerstrasse, very near to Checkpoint Charlie, and had been hit by a bullet fired by a GDR Border Guard. He bled to death at the foot of the Wall on East German territory; neither the West Berlin Police nor the allied soldiers felt that they could offer him first aid.

1973

The question of free access to the city remained a stumbling block in relations between East and West, the GDR and the Federal Republic. The only way of getting to Berlin without going through customs and passport controls was by air. The road and rail connections were always being threatened with disruption and already such events as the election of Gustav Heinemann to the Federal Presidency in March 1969, which was supposed to take place in the Reichstag, had been used by the GDR as a reason to temporarily block the transit routes. West Berlin's integration with the West and its ties with the Federal Republic, as demonstrated by the meeting of the Federal Convention in the city, were a thorn in the GDR Government's side. The Federal Republic steadfastly refused to recognise the GDR as a sovereign state and the West continued to maintain the view that Berlin was a Four Sector city under the jurisdiction of the Allies.

The insistence on this position finally led to the Four Power Agreement on Berlin at the beginning of the seventies and to the first noticeable thaw in German-German relations. A new departure was that now the Soviet Union was responsible for getting civilian traffic smoothly into West Berlin and consequently it became possible to transport goods in sealed lorries down the transit routes, without the need for customs checks. Visitors only had to produce identity and no longer had to pay anything (this was paid for centrally by the Federal Republic). Thorough checks would only be carried out if there was any cause for suspicion. On the other hand, the Western Allies limited the number of Federal events in West Berlin. The election of the Federal President could no longer take place and even plenary meetings of the Bundestag (Federal Parliament) or the Bundesrat (Upper House) were not permitted.

The most renowned special ruling for Berlin was its demilitarisation. Germans with permanent residency in Berlin (West) could not do military service and over the years this meant that Berlin attracted many young men who wanted to avoid conscription; they couldn't even be contacted by post because the Allies prohibited the distribution of conscription papers. The GDR authorities did not take the demilitarisation – which the Allies had agreed to apply to both halves of the city – as seriously. The army legislation there, which introduced National Service in 1965, also included young East Berliners. Protests from the Federal Government, the West Berlin Senate and the Western Allies proved fruitless.

The last important step towards German-German détente was the "Grundlagenvertrag" (Foundations Treaty) between the two governments which came into force on 21st June 1973.

A significant and visible consequence for Berlin was the setting up of a "Ständige Vertretung" (permanent representation) of the Embassy of the Federal Republic in the GDR. Its name indicated that Bonn was still insisting on a special relationship but wouldn't stand in the way of a quasi dual nation state any longer.

The Dual City

West Berlin's island position had far-reaching effects. It wasn't just the fact that when the Wall went up companies lost thousands of employees overnight, many young people, particularly those with qualifications, simply left West Berlin. There was not only a decrease in the population but more importantly, there was a change in its composition. The city was suffering from being too old and therefore from a lack of people of working age and advertised for workers from the Federal Republic or even from abroad. In many ways this laid the foundation stone for today's multi-cultural Berlin which would be unthinkable without large foreign communities. The decline in West Berlin's population was partly compensated for by the influx of foreigners. By the end of 1989 the largest group was the Turks with 128,000, followed by the Yugoslavians and Poles.

Despite the shock of the Wall, cultural and social life slowly began to recover as well. In 1963 the Philharmonie (Philharmonic Concert Hall) on Kemperplatz, designed by Hans Sharoun, was officially opened and was the first building of the planned Kulturforum (Cultural Forum). Striking architectural projects, including the Neue Nationalgalerie (New National Gallery) designed by Mies van der Rohe or the Staatsbibliothek (State Library) also by Sharoun, all bore the hallmark of a divided city; they were clearly seen as alternatives to the historical centre around Unter den Linden. The dual structure of Berlin now began to make itself felt in all aspects of life.

In East Berlin there were also attempts to introduce new architectural trends. The main purpose of the 365 metre high television tower on Alexanderplatz, completed in 1969 and one of the tallest buildings in Europe, was to advertise the achievements of socialism. All around Alexanderplatz appeared new inner-city residential developments dissected by broad avenues and which today still retain something of the atmosphere of a socialist city. The Palast der Republik (East

Rudi Dutschke (centre) at a demonstration, 1967.

Squatters demonstrate in West Berlin, 1980.

Berlin Parliament) opened in 1976 and built partly on the site of the former Stadtschloss, opposite the Berliner Dom (Berlin Cathedral) had the same feel about it, and inside it was the architectural gem of the GDR capital, the "Haus des Volkes" where the East German parliament met and which contained restaurants and other forms of entertainment to attract large numbers of visitors.

Thus it was possible in the dual city to complete the architectural development that had been started at the turn of the century. Since this time Berlin had had *de facto* two city centres; one round the Kurfürstendamm, the central point for the chic world of the new west and the other between Alexanderplatz and the boulevard of Unter den Linden, the centre of cultural and political life. In West Berlin, the Zoologischer Garter station and the Café Kranzler on the corner of Joachimstaler Strasse and Kurfürstendamm were now the symbols of city life, whilst the political centre with the seat of the Mayor of West Berlin moved out to Schöneberg. In East Berlin, the favourite meeting place was the international clock on Alexanderplatz and people took their city stroll past the Rotes Rathaus to the Palast der Republik.

Both social life as well as cultural life developed quite differently in each half of the city. As the largest university city in Germany, West Berlin had been a stronghold of the student movement since the late sixties and in February 1966 it was here that the first Vietnam demonstration against the Americans took place. The death of Benno Ohnesorg, who was shot by the police on 2nd June 1967 at a demonstration against the visit of the Shah of Persia, turned the student protests into a mass movement that soon exerted considerable influence on political life all over the Federal Republic as the APO (Ausserparlamentarische Opposition – the opposition from outside parliament). On 1st May 1968 40,000 supporters of the APO took to the streets after one of their leaders, Rudi Dutschke, was seriously injured during an assassination attempt on the Kurfürstendamm. The centre of student protest became the Free University of Berlin in Dahlem, whose existence was closely linked with the division of the city. It was founded in 1948 when professors, lecturers and students wanted to disassociate themselves from the political pressure put on them by the Humboldt-Universität in the Soviet Sector.

Parade on 20th Anniversary of the GDR on 7th October 1969.

It was also in West Berlin that the APO first split into moderate and radical wings. A terrorist group formed whose members began to wage an armed war against the Federal Republic. Their first most spectacular action was when Ulrike Meinhof and her accomplices used force to free Andreas Baader from the Tegel detention centre.

In East Berlin, opposition to the SED Party State developed quite differently. Robert Havemann, Professor for Physical Chemistry at the Humboldt-Universität, became the figurehead for the dissidents there when he was summarily dismissed from his post in 1964 for his critical remarks. He was then banned from his profession, placed under Stasi surveillance, confined to his home and subjected to other means of repression. Until his death in 1982, he continued to campaign for a more democratic form of socialism and used the media in the West to try and influence social development in the GDR. The song-writer and singer Wolf Biermann (born 1936), one of the most well-known East German dissidents, lived in East Berlin and was a close friend of Havemann's. GDR writers and artists launched a series of protest campaigns after Biermann was exiled from the GDR in 1976 whilst he was away on an authorised tour of the Federal Republic. However the opposition movement did not manage to attract a broader base until the eighties, not long before the GDR collapsed.

In the seventies West Berlin became a Mecca for young people who wanted to lead an alternative style of life and experiment with communes, run their own left-wing playgroups and alternative businesses. In 1981 the political wing of this alternative scene, the Alternative Liste (AL) gained 7.2

percent of the vote and had seats in the Abgeordnetenhaus (West Berlin House of Representatives) for the first time.

A particular characteristic of life in West Berlin in the eighties was the active squatters' scene which had started in 1979 as a protest against the shortage of housing and the way in which speculators left houses standing empty. In 1984 the number of buildings occupied by squatters was reduced to twelve by issuing contracts granting their use.

Both halves of the city made mistakes in urban development. In West and East Berlin wholesale clearing of old buildings took place; stucco façades were "smoothed down" and damaged buildings were replaced with modern ones. Satellite towns were a new feature of life on both sides of the Wall. They were supposed to offer an improved quality of living but instead often brought unforeseen social problems for their inhabitants. West Berlin built the Märkisches Viertel and the Gropiusstadt in Neukölln and a little later Hellersdorf and Marzahn were constructed in East Berlin, using the characteristic pre-fabricated slabs.

In 1987 the separate halves of Berlin (yet still united by their common history) celebrated the 750th Anniversary of their city with particular emphasis on their new plans for urban development. In East Berlin it was an opportunity to launch a district which had been reconstructed in the old style – the Nicolai Viertel. Houses made of modern materials, partly using pre-fabricated slabs were built around oldest church in the city, the Nicolai Kirche, and were intended to evoke the aura of the medieval town. "Genuine" old buildings were included, for example the "Zum Nussbaum" inn, which the artist Heinrich Zille used to frequent,

1987

although back in those days it used to stand a few hundred metres away on Fischerinsel. West Berlin organised an International Building Competition to mark the 750th Anniversary and invited renowned architects from all over the world to build houses in various inner-city districts following the basic principles of good social urban development.

The Fall of the Wall

Berlin remained a city divided by force. During the eighties the border installations were further perfected, even if within the GDR the opposition movement had been strengthened. One of the centres for the opposition was East Berlin, especially in a district like Prenzlauer Berg. Here the dissidents met up under the protection of church groups or they became environmentalists collecting information about environmental destruction in the GDR. Politically active groups in both East and West Germany shared a common cause in their resistance against the arms race between Nato and the Warsaw Pact. In the GDR, "Swords into ploughshares", became the most famous slogan of this movement. In the meantime economic problems were making the GDR increasingly unstable, even the authorised emigration waves of the eighties did nothing to relieve the situation at home.
Whilst the SED leadership under Erich Honecker made preparations for the 40th Anniversary of the GDR on 7th October 1989, most citizens were in no mood to celebrate this event. Instead they gave a rousing welcome to the Soviet premier Michail Gorbatschow, whose Glasnost and

Berliners on top of the Wall at Brandenburg Gate, 10th November 1989.

Perestroika were signs of hope for the peaceful liberalisation and democratisation of Eastern Europe. On 18th October 1989 Honecker resigned as Leader of the State and the Party; his successor was Egon Krenz, but by now it was the people themselves who were in charge. On 4th November a million GDR citizens assembled on Alexanderplatz in the biggest demonstration in the history of their country. Their unanimous demands were for freedom of the press, freedom of assembly and freedom of speech. Many of their prominent figures like the actor, Ulrich Mühe or the writer, Christa Wolf, spoke up for the Democracy Movement.

However, the decisive moment came a few days later on 9th November when Günter Schabowski, a member of the Politbüro (SED cabinet) casually announced at a press conference that the requirement for a visa to leave the GDR had been lifted and when pressed for further clarification by an Italian journalist, he said that this ruling took immediate effect. The press conference was being broadcast live on GDR and after the news programme "Tagesschau" in the West joined in and announced, "GDR opens its borders", thousands of East Berliners set off for the inner-city checkpoints. A few hours later the border guards were no longer able to withstand the vociferous demand to "Let us out", coming from all sides. At 22.30 the barrier was raised at the checkpoint between Prenzlauer Berg and Wedding and shortly after midnight all the checkpoints were open. The Wall had fallen.

The Hackeschen Höfe by night. Photo by Andreas Muhs, 2000.

The New Centre

Berlin after the Fall of the Wall

A time of new departures

In the days and weeks following the fall of the Wall the city was in turmoil. Hundreds of thousands of visitors flooded to West Berlin and to the Federal Republic and the S-Bahn, underground, busses and streets were packed with people. Long queues of GDR citizens formed outside banks to collect their "welcome money" (100 DM per person). People began to break down the Wall all over the city. On 12th November one of the first provisional crossing points was set up at Potsdamer Platz, where members of the border troops had removed several sections of the Wall during the night. In the morning the two Berlin Mayors, Walter Momper (West) and Erhard Krack (East) were able to walk up to one another at this central meeting point in the former capital of Germany. In the years to follow, Potsdamer Platz became an example of how infra-structure divided for so long can be joined together again. At first it was pedestrians who streamed across from one side to the other and soon came the cars. In March 1992 the S-Bahn station at Potsdamer Platz was re-opened, quickly followed by the Underground and then bus number 2 coming from Zoo Station, was once again able to continue its route towards Alexanderplatz via the stations at Mohrenstrasse and Stadtmitte.

The four Allies from World War II were once again required in order to safeguard the political future of Berlin. In the so-called "Two plus Four Negotiations" in February 1990, held in Ottawa, Canada, the course was set for a united and free Germany. The negotiations finally allowed the GDR to join the Federal Republic on 3rd October 1990 in accordance with the decision of the GDR parliament. When the "Two plus Four Talks" ended in September of the same year in Moscow, the four victorious powers relinquished their rights all over Germany and within four years they had withdrawn all their occupying troops from the city of Berlin, officially ending its Four Power Status. The inner-city border installations had already been removed a good year after the fall of the Wall as a visible sign of reunification.

On 2nd December 1990 for the first time in decades Berliners jointly took part both in elections for the Bundestag and for the Berlin House of Representatives (Abgeordnetenhaus). The result in Berlin was a grand SPD/CDU coalition and Eberhard Diepgen, as elected Mayor, was once again able to take up his seat in the Rotes Rathaus in Berlin-Mitte. The next highly significant step for

Berlin was the decision of the Bundestag in June 1991 to make Berlin the capital of reunited Germany. In September 1999 the German Bundestag was finally able to hold its first sitting in the restored Reichstag building, designed by Sir Norman Foster. The dome became a symbol of the new Berlin Republic, as well as a favourite tourist spot with a commanding view of the rapidly changing city centre.

In the last decade of the 20th Century Berlin was mainly a city of building sites. "Everything is on the move", Martin Kessel had said over 70 years previously in his Berlin novel, "Herr Brecher's Fiasko". "It is in Berlin's fugitive character that it has managed to have an official centre which no-one could describe as a focal point." Today Berlin has once again created an "official" centre, the new government district with the Chancellory, offices for Members of Parliament, the seat of the Federal President and numerous ministries, embassies and press agencies from all over the world. But the heart of Berlin is stylized by Potsdamer Platz; here were the links with the myths of the lost metropolis and this was the area where the new projects for urban and architectural concepts were developed. The big investors in Potsdamer Platz were the DaimlerChrylser subsidiaries in the area south of Potsdamer Strasse as well as the Japanese media concern Sony to the north of it. Over the years of its construction, building progress on the site could be followed from a red information box built above Leipziger Platz.

If Berlin had lost one of its tourist attractions with the Wall, it gained a new one with all the huge building sites. In fact there are only very few remnants of the former inner city border to be found, often even Berliners themselves cannot state with any certainty where exactly the Wall once stood. In the central area a line has been drawn along the streets to make the route clear and a short section of the Wall can be viewed by the Martin Gropius building in Niederkirchnerstrasse and in Bernauer Strasse in Wedding, where there is also a memorial and a Berlin Wall Documentation Centre. But perhaps the most impressive remnant is the long stretch of Wall by the Spree, between Ostbahnhof and Oberbaumbrücke, better known as East Side Gallery where in the spring of 1990, 118 artists from all over the world celebrated peace and the end of a divided Europe with extensive wall-paintings.

Perspectives for the New Millenium

In the wake of reunification East and West Berlin were brought together again by the fact that they both experienced economic problems. Whilst in the East numerous big companies who could not compete in a market economy were wound up, in the West it was firms that had only survived with the help of subsidies. By the mid-nineties the number of jobs in industry had been halved and since then the rate of unemployment has remained correspondingly high and local government equally in debt. A large proportion of the taxes went towards repaying the interest and an attempt to create new structures and scope for action by amalgamating the Federal States of Berlin and Brandenburg failed at a referendum held in 1996.

One clear sign that the political-administrative division has been overcome was

Under the glass dome of the Reichstag building. Photograph by Andreas Muhs, 1999.

the election for the House of Representatives in October 2001 where the Social Democrats (SPD) were declared the winners although with only 29.7 percent of the second vote they gained less than 20 percent under an absolute majority. The Christian Democrats (CDU) lagged behind them with under a quarter of the votes (23.7 percent) and the Party of Democratic Socialists (PDS) followed with a fifth (22.6 percent) of the votes. After lengthy negotiations a coalition made up of the SPD and PDS was set up and Social Democrat Klaus Wowereit was elected as the new Mayor. Only a few years before, it would have been unthinkable for the PDS, a party that had emerged from the dissolution of the SED, to be involved in any power sharing. Now it seemed the only way forward if large sections of the population were not to be excluded from democratic participation.

After the party atmosphere which followed the fall of the Wall, the over-optimistic hopes for economic development of the city began to fade. Only a few large companies came to Berlin, mainly service and media industries. Berlin remains a city with an attractive location and an image which companies want to associate with, but where nothing much is produced and there is no serious investment.

Berlin continues to attract young creative people from all over the world and this is reflected in the large numbers of visitors, especially from within Europe. Big events such as the Love Parade, the Christopher Street Day or the Carnival of Cultures, which for many years have filled the streets of Berlin with an increasing number of people, have played a large part in the city's image.

Life in certain city districts has changed considerably in the course of the nineties. The borough of Kreuzberg, once the centre of the in-scene and for all drop-outs, now seems rather a quiet area, although it has long cast off the shadow of the Wall. Today it is districts like Prenzlauer Berg or Friedrichshain that have become really "in" and where the nightlife in cafés, pubs, bars and clubs is concentrated. Even the arrival of so many government workers from Bonn hasn't really had a lasting effect on the character of the city. There are, of course, a lot more smart areas, restaurants and bars but there is enough room for everyone in the city. If the streets between Oranienburger Strasse and the Hackesche Markt in the Mitte district seem too tourist-orientated and false, the genuine Berlin ambiance can be found just a few blocks round the corner.

With the continuing expansion of the EU Berlin is developing once more into a meeting point between East and West and the city remains true to its tradition as a place for immigrants. In the decades preceding the Second World War the Russian community was over a hundred thousand strong and now it is rapidly growing again. Berlin is also a great attraction for nearby Poland with whom it has strong economic ties and enjoys an exchange of workers and services.

The past century has probably seen Berlin's most dramatic development: from Imperial capital to centre of the Greater German Reich, from island city to a great metropolis in a united Europe. One thing is certain – Berlin has a wealth of experience on which to build its future.

Potsdamer Platz with its traffic tower, about 1930.

Chronological Table

c. 700 A.D. Slav tribes settle on the land which later becomes Berlin.

1134 Askanier Prince, Albrecht the Bear becomes Margrave of the North March (Markgraf der Nordmark).

1237 Berlin's sister town, Cölln, is first mentioned in a document.

1244 Berlin is first mentioned in document

1417 Friedrich I of the Hollenzollern (1371–1440) is named Margrave and Elector.

1443 The first Stadtschloss (City Palace) is built on the banks of the Spree.

1539 The Reformation comes to Berlin.

1618–1648 Berlin loses a third of its population in the Thirty Years War.

1685 The Edict of Potsdam grants the immigration of Huguenots, Protestant refugees from France, who settle mainly in Berlin.

1701 The son of the Great Elector, Friedrich I (1657–1713) is crowned King of Prussia.

1738 The beginning of the building of the Akzise Wall as the customs border of the city.

1791 The Brandenburg Gate, designed by the architect, Karl Gotthard Langhans and adorned with the Quadriga by Gottfried Schadow, is opened to the public.

1802 The Schauspielhaus opens on Gendarmenmarkt.

1806 French occupation troops under Napoleon march into the city through the Brandenburg Gate.

1810 Friedrich Wilhelm University is founded.

1837 August Borsig founds a workshop which quickly becomes one of Germany's most important engineering works.

1838 The first Prussian railway line links Berlin with Potsdam.

1848 Revolutionary battles at the barricades cost over 200 lives.

1865 The license for the first horse-drawn train between Charlottenburg and Kupfergraben is granted.

1871 The German Empire is proclaimed, with Berlin as its capital.

1873 The construction of a modern sewerage system is started, designed by James Hobrecht.

1881 The first electric tram goes into service between Lichterfelde Ost station and the Kadettenanstalt.

1902 Berlin is the fifth large European city (after London, Budapest, Glasgow and Paris) to have an underground railway.

1907 The KaDeWe (Kaufhaus des Westens) department store opens on Tauentzienstrasse, Charlottenburg.

1918 The end of the First World War. Abdication of Kaiser Wilhelm I.

1919 The Spartacus uprising and murder of Karl Liebknecht and Rosa Luxemburg.

1920 A law on the formation of a new municipality of Berlin is passed, Greater Berlin now consists of seven neighbouring towns and 59 country communities.

1924 Berlin's first traffic signals are erected on Potsdamer Platz.

1930 Marlene Dietrich celebrates a triumphant success with her film „The Blue Angel".

1932 The anti-democratic parties, including the KPD (Communists) and the NSDAP (Nazis) gain an absolute majority in the Reichstag elections in November.

1933 Adolf Hitler celebrates his appointment as Reichskanzler (Chancellor of Germany) with a torchlight procession through the Brandenburg Gate.

1936 The Olympic Games are used by the National Socialists for propaganda purposes.

1937 Berlin celebrates its 700th Anniversary.

1938 Pogrom during the night of 9/10th November.

1944 After the assassination attempt of 20th July scores of resistance fighters are arrested and executed.

1945 Hitler commits suicide in his bunker under the Chancellory. At the Potsdam Conference from 17th July to 2nd August the leaders of the three great powers, USA, USSR and Great Britain discuss the future of Germany.

1948 The blockade of the three Western Sectors and the start of the Berlin Airlift.

1949 The introduction of the Basic Law in the Federal Republic and the founding of the German Democratic Republic is the beginning of German dual sovereignty.

1953 Soviet troops have to be brought in to quell the uprising on 17th June.

1961 The Berlin Wall is erected on 13th August.

1967 Benno Ohnesorg is shot dead by a West Berlin policeman during a demonstration against the visit of the Shah of Persia.

1987 The 750th Anniversary of Berlin is celebrated separately in each half of the city.

1989 Erich Honecker resigns as leader of the SED and the GDR. On 9th November the checkpoints are opened and the Wall falls.

1991 The German Bundestag makes the decision to move the capital to Berlin.

1999 The first sitting of the Bundestag in the restored Reichstag building.

2001 After the October election for the Berlin House of Representatives, the Party of Democratic Socialism (PDS) forms part of the coalition with the SPD.

Bibliography

Arnold, Dietmar: Der Potsdamer Platz von unten. Eine Zeitreise durch dunkle Welten. Berlin 2001.

Bade, Wilfrid: Die SA erobert Berlin. Ein Tatsachenbericht. München 1933.

Cullen, Michael S.: Der Reichstag. Parlament, Denkmal, Symbol. Berlin 1999.

Dietrich, Richard (Hrsg.): Berlin. Zehn Kapitel seiner Geschichte. Berlin 1981.

Döblin, Alfred: Berlin Alexanderplatz. Die Geschichte vom Franz Biberkopf. München 1965 [EA 1929].

Drexel, Gerhard: Rund um den Gendarmenmarkt. Berlin 2001.

Flemming, Thomas: Kein Tag der deutschen Einheit. 17. Juni 1953. Berlin 2003.

Ders.; Hagen Koch: Die Berliner Mauer. Geschichte eines politischen Bauwerks. Berlin 1999.

Fromm, Eberhard; Hans-Jürgen Mende (Hrsg.): 800 Jahre Berlin-Geschichte Tag für Tag. Berlin 1996.

Gewiese, Armin; Ulrike Dömeland: Durch Berlin mit dem Schiff. Berlin 2003.

Görtemaker, Manfred: Weimar in Berlin. Porträt einer Epoche. Berlin 2002.

Kessel, Martin: Herrn Brechers Fiasko. Frankfurt/M. 2001 [EA 1932].

Ladwig-Winters, Simone: Wertheim. Geschichte eines Warenhauses. Berlin 1997.

Large, David Clay: Berlin. Biographie einer Stadt. München 2002.

Leonhard, Wolfgang: Die Revolution entlässt ihre Kinder. Köln 1955.

Lummel, Peter (Hrsg.): Kaffee. Vom Schmuggelgut zum Lifestyle-Klassiker. Drei Jahrhunderte Berliner Kaffeekultur. Berlin 2002.

Meyer-Kronthaler, Jürgen; Klaus Kurpjuweit: Berliner U-Bahn. In Fahrt seit hundert Jahren. Berlin 2001.

Ribbe, Wolfgang; Jürgen Schmädeke: Kleine Berlin-Geschichte. Berlin 1988.

Ribbe, Wolfgang (Hrsg.): Geschichte Berlins. 1. Bd. Von der Frühgeschichte bis zur Industrialisierung. München 1987.

Ders.: Geschichte Berlins. 2. Bd. Von der Märzrevolution bis zur Gegenwart. München 1987.

Schoeps, Julius H. (Hrsg.): Berlin. Geschichte einer Stadt. Berlin 2001.

Ders.: Preußen. Geschichte eines Mythos. Berlin 2000.

Strohmeyer, Klaus (Hrsg.): Berlin in Bewegung. Literarischer Spaziergang 1. Die Berliner. Hamburg 1987.

Ders.: Berlin in Bewegung. Literarischer Spaziergang 2. Die Stadt. Hamburg 1987.

Vogel, Werner: Führer durch die Geschichte Berlins. Berlin 1993.

Winteroll, Michael: Die Geschichte Berlins. Ein Stadtführer durch die Jahrhunderte. Berlin 2002.

Zur Mühlen, Bengt von; Frank Bauer, Karen Pfundt, Tony Le Tissier: Der Todeskampf der Reichshauptstadt. Berlin, Kleinmachnow 1994.